SONS OF AFRICA

SONS OF AFRICA

by

GEORGINA A. GOLLOCK

Former Joint Editor of the *International
Review of Missions*. Author of *Lives
of Eminent Africans, etc.*

Decorations by
AARON DOUGLAS

FRIENDSHIP PRESS
New York

MV
920
G62
(2)

RIND. 17 Ma '37

TO MY FRIEND

JAMES EMMAN KWEGYIR AGGREY
*of Salisbury, North Carolina, and of
Achimota College, Gold Coast*
WHO IN LIFE AND DEATH
LINKED AFRICA AND NORTH AMERICA
TOGETHER

CONTENTS

PREFACE

THE first chapter of this book is really its preface, setting forth in full its genesis and its aim. But it remains to acknowledge here the generous help given from many countries, notably from North America, in the preparation and presentation of material. Government officials, missionaries, and others with knowledge either of African history or of the Africans whose stories are here told, have never wearied in giving counsel and aid. In particular several African friends, women and men, have in my own home gone over parts of the book with me, rendering service which no others could have given.

Mention must be made by name of several friends to whom special thanks are due, though I cannot shift my responsibility for what has been written to their shoulders. They are Canon Anson Phelps Stokes and Dr. T. Jesse Jones of the Phelps-Stokes Fund; Dr. C. T. Loram, Commissioner of Native Affairs in the Union of South Africa; the Rev. Edwin W. Smith, author of *The Golden Stool,* who was kind enough to

read the book in manuscript; and the late Dr.
J. E. K. Aggrey, who only a few weeks before
his death guided the choice of African characters for these pages and lit the flame of his own
enthusiasm in the writer's mind.

The resources of the fine Library of the Royal
Colonial Institute in London, including many
rare books on Africa, have been always at my
service, together with the expert advice of the
Librarian and his staff. From first to last the
work of collaboration with the officers of the
Missionary Education Movement has been as easy
and almost as swift as if no ocean rolled between. One and all they leave me gratefully in
their debt.

GEORGINA A. GOLLOCK

London
May 1928

SONS OF AFRICA

I. THE DISCOVERY OF THE SONS OF AFRICA

THE discovery of Africa in the geographical sense is almost complete; its material resources, the riches of mine and forest and field, are being rapidly explored. Men are finding out that if the physical wealth of the continent is to be garnered, the human wealth must be conserved. The balance sheet of a colony depends upon the birth-rate; income is affected by infant mortality; wealth in colonial coffers depends on health in African kraals. This discovery has led, of course, to increased care of the Africans. So far so good. But to care for men as tools which are to be kept in good order that better work may be done by them, or even to educate them that being happier they may live longer and do more productive work, is not enough. The discovery of the African as a means to the white man's ends begins to yield place to the greater discovery that the African is an end in himself.

This discovery as yet is far from complete. But over a wide area it has been begun, not only by missionaries and philanthropists but by individual men representing government departments both in Africa and in colonial offices, and by certain pioneers of commerce and trade from the Old World and the New. There are settlers face to face with the problem of local labor who are resolved to seek its solution on lines that will uplift and develop the African; and there are travelers, publicists, scientists, writers, who have caught a glimpse of the African as a man among men.

No discovery is mere guess-work. It calls for careful exploration and detailed record of fact. There is no gain in evaluation of the human wealth of Africa by a one-eyed man who can believe no ill of his fellow-creatures. The African must stand on no artificial eminence, but on a level with other races, judged by the standards applicable to them at the same stage of development. Common sense and science, not sentiment, must govern research. Unsupported generalizations about racial characteristics are futile and dangerous indulgences.

But if what some men believe they are discovering as to the worth and capacity of the African is true, then the face of African affairs must change. The African himself will be saved by hope, and will rise to new and disciplined endeavor. The selfish white man will repent his grasping; the haughty white man will blush to recall his scorn. The last vestige of the whip will fall from the hand of the overseer, as compulsion to work is replaced by cooperation of white and black in mutual respect towards a common end.

About two hundred Americans and Europeans, gathered in Belgium for a week of residential conference on the Christian Mission in Africa, made a stride towards discovery of the sons of Africa in the autumn of 1926. Government administrators, leading educationalists and doctors, colonial officials of various grades, students of racial problems, and many missionaries were there. Most of the members had lived in Africa; all had knowledge of African affairs. A full and frank presentation of African problems—political, racial, economic, social, educational and religious—had been circulated in advance. No member came seeing a clear way through the maze. But before the week was over, hope was born. It came in the form not of plan but of personality.

There was present a small group of Africans, mostly well known, from several tribes. There was also a larger group of Negroes from the

United States. All were proven men and women, delegated by responsible organizations. In conversation, in recreation, and in worship, an atmosphere was created in which burning questions were handled through long hours of discussion with naturalness and ease. There was no self-consciousness on either side. Equality? It was neither challenged nor affirmed. Racial difference ceased to be a barrier and became an enrichment and widening of contribution, the addition of elements of high essential value to the common store. Each race speaking with perfect freedom welcomed free speech in return. The discovery made by the white members was—the Africans. And in a delightful mutuality the Africans discovered us.

It is well said in the biography of Stewart of Lovedale that the discovery of one great diamond indicates diamondiferous soil; the other stones may be smaller, yet the quality may be the same. The Belgian conference raised the question whether in the broad records of African tribal history other diamonds were to be found. Was there evidence of a wider distribution of capacity for cooperation and leadership than had generally been recognized? In other words, was it rational to believe that Africans were as great an asset for the world as was Africa itself?

In search of an answer to that question the writer has spent a year of close work. Such study as occasion offered has been made of living African friends, both women and men. The writings of historians, travelers, administrators, scientists, traders, and missionaries have been drawn upon. Dusty old journals have been sought out on library shelves. Material throwing light on individual Africans and their qualities has been amassed. A steady effort has been made to arrive at truth. Where possible, information has been gathered from those who have known individual Africans well.

The individuals selected for study have ranged in time from the fifteenth century to today; in rank from kings and great potentates down to simple evangelists, school teachers and small tribal chiefs; in moral qualities from a warrior like Tshaka to Khama the Good. They have ranged from a great administrator like Sir Apolo Kagwa to Livingstone's faithful servants; from a cultured and traveled educationalist like Dr. J. E. K. Aggrey to an intrepid evangelist who knows no English but who has built a living church; from women like the queen-mothers of Ashanti and Uganda or the famous "Female Elephant," queen of Swaziland, to the host of good wives and mothers who made the men of Africa, and to the women evangelists, nurses, and teachers who are serving successive African generations.

It has been an absorbing study. There has been the background of Africa, pagan or Moslem, full of strange beauty, always touched with shadow, sometimes dark with superstition and pain. There has been the nearness of that haunting primitive life which surrounded our own ancestors centuries ago. There has been the social miasma from groups of stagnant, decadent, dispossessed people, more extensive though far less reprehensible than similar plague spots in the West. A sickening sense of evil has been left by records of white men who have accelerated the degradation of the African, of places where African savagery and vice have held sway. There has been the crudeness of racial adolescence; the evidence of racial awakening to issues not fully understood. But through all, the discovery of the sons of Africa has grown more clear. Characters of real beauty, of solid worth and outstanding capacity, have constantly emerged. In men and

women obviously far from perfect, characteristics of rich significance have been found.

It is dangerous to attempt to classify the noteworthy African qualities which this study has
revealed, for to some minds one local instance
to the contrary confutes a generalization however widely based. But there are subjects on
which caution is akin to cowardice, and I will
venture to be rash.

Fidelity to a trust that has been undertaken,
and patience, were put forward as outstanding
African qualities by Sir Gordon Guggisberg in
his last address as Governor of the Gold Coast.
Evidence confirming his long and wide experience has constantly come to hand. Israel in
Egypt did not surpass the African in endurance:
witness his survival through the harrowing of
the slave trade. Yet, unlike the Jew, the African is easily depressed by distrust. He tends to
become what he is believed to be. Capacity for
administrative work, quickness in seeing situations, and acumen in adjudicating on them, are
more common among eminent Africans than is
generally recognized. These qualities may of
course be vitiated by moral weakness, but their
distribution is fairly wide. Power to acquire
knowledge quickly and correctly is supple-

mented by unusually retentive memory. Perception and adaptability in social life are marked, and go far deeper than mere imitativeness. An African even in strange surroundings seldom makes a mistake. Courage, both physical and moral, is shown in endurance and in boldness of attack; it is a tribal virtue which has notably taken root in the Christian church. Tenacity of purpose is also strong. Industry is to a high degree characteristic of African life under normal conditions. It is marked in all Africans who have become known as great. Idleness, as a rule, belongs to the vicious or the dispossessed who have been torn from old surroundings. Kindliness, hospitality and generosity are, as every missionary and traveler knows, at home in Africa; there are exceptions, as even Livingstone learned. Humor is quite widespread. Sometimes it is the exuberant fun and merriment of a child, but it may, as in the case of a man like Dr. Aggrey, take the form of brilliant and penetrating wit. The African's sense of humor reinforces his patience in a remarkable way. In eloquence, in repartee, in art, in music, in the dance, he finds opportunity to use his gifts of expression. Though there are notable instances to the contrary, grateful remembrance is an attractive feature in African mentality. Finally, to an extent unknown in the West, the religious sense is dominating and pervasive; an African is full of wonder; the whole of his life is in touch with a spirit world. While customs with religious content pass unchanged from age to age, the Western association of religion with mere theological formulæ is unnatural to the African; unhappily, however, it is sometimes acquired.

Here, at the outset, belief has been avowed in the sons of Africa, and the value of their discovery for the world. It is only the echo of what David Livingstone said. In his day there were few Africans who had acquired higher education or qualified themselves for professional work. There was then no opportunity for a Bantu in the south to share in administrative work with the whites. Few of the African friends of Livingstone could read and write. Yet he discovered their qualities and proclaimed them to the world. "I have no fears," he once said in addressing an English audience, "as to the mental and moral capacity of the Africans for civilization and upward progress. I who have been intimate with Africans believe them to be capable of holding an honorable place in the family of man."

In the chapters that follow, in only one or two instances has an attempt to argue the case been made. Some of the stories which recent study has made living have been told. Those who read may find in them confirmation of what has here been said. If they do not, it will be the telling of the stories that has failed. The evidence in the lives of the men is indubitable.

II. THE GREAT ASKIA: A TALE OF TIMBUKTU

IN the middle of the fifteenth century there was born on an island in the Niger, not far from Timbuktu, a baby boy with no special pretensions to greatness, who was to usurp a throne and found one of the famous dynasties of the western Sudan. His background is one of those thrilling chapters of medieval history which are easily forgotten in the rush of modern events in Africa.

In the seventh century of the Christian era the victorious Arabs, flushed with the passion of their new religion of Islam, spread across northern Africa. In the early years of the eighth century they carried out successful expeditions against the Mediterranean islands, in particular Sicily; then they pushed across to Spain. The Straits of Gibraltar ceased to be a barrier and became a bridge.

In the train of the Arabs came that rich culture and love of learning which has been the wonder of each succeeding age. Between the barbarism, or at best the superstitious ignorance, of pagan African tribes to the south, and the rude strength of European tribes—many still pagan—to the north, lay the belt of Arab civilization, full of life. Incorporating much of the Berber life of Africa, the Arabs carried it onward with them into Spain. In turn they brought Spain back with them into Africa. The Moorish kingdom which the Arabs set up was known as Adouatein, the empire of the two shores, one being European, one African. Twice during the long-continued Moorish dominance African dynasties reigned over the court in Spain.

Arab civilization and commerce also spread southward across the sandy desert—a caravan journey of from forty to fifty days. Imagination turns again and again, unsated, to the mystery and solitude of those ancient desert tracks, the most permanent of all means of communication, which are still as they were a thousand years ago. One main route strikes southward through Tripoli, forking to Lake Chad on the east and to Khago or Gao on the bend of the Niger on the west. The other main route pushes southward through Morocco; it is the caravan road to Timbuktu.

Standing in that great town on the Niger, the

men of the Middle Ages looking southward
thought of regions occupied by hordes of sav-
ages and cannibals, good only to be captured as
slaves. There were the Dem-Dem and Rem-
Rem, and further east the Gnem-Gnem, as the
old maps show. They little dreamed that one
day these lands would be well-ordered colonies,
Nigeria and the rest, with growing Christian
churches and races capable of playing a full part
in the world's life. In the days of which we
write, the outlet of the heart of Central Africa
was northward towards Spain or eastward
towards Egypt. From north and east, too, came
the inflow of new life. Portugal had already,
however, in Sonni Ali's days, begun through the
enterprise of King John II to make an approach.
Later on, other countries of Europe began to
press inward from the west and south to trade.

The romance of the desert and of the great
fertile areas south of it met in Timbuktu, the
city of the canoe and the camel. To it, borne
up or down the great river or through num-
berless converging waterways, canoes brought
products of agriculture and industry from the
south. It was the mart to which the northern
desert sent by camel its priceless riches of salt,
its dates, its strange wild wares.

Old and half-forgotten records [1] picture the coming of strangers to the city, with its mud-built walls, the mingled magnificence and squalor of its life, the trade of its merchants, the learning in its libraries, the worship in its mosques. Then the Moors, expelled from Spain in 1502, degenerated to the mere pursuit of war and swept like a curtain of mist across the scene, obliterating the kingdoms which were acting and reacting on one another, and veiling the Sudan for centuries from the rest of the world. Travelers in later years, when the glory of the city had departed, tried to repeople the past, writing of "Timbuktu the Mysterious," and in its ruins and half-ruins have found remnants of former prosperity.

In this city of Timbuktu, with this background of history, is set the figure of the first son of Africa whom we select for study, Mohammed Abu Bekr Et-Tourti, the founder of the Askia dynasty, and the builder of the greatest days of the Songhay empire.

He was born, as already stated, on an island in the Niger. He was a full-blooded black of well known family. His father was widely re-

[1] Lady Lugard has gathered from all available sources material for her delightful book, *A Tropical Dependency* (1905), on which this chapter is largely based. The book is, unfortunately, out of print.

spected; his mother was a pious Moslem and cared for her children well; one of his brothers was said to be "black in color, but most beautiful in mind and conditions." As a boy and throughout his life Mohammed was an orthodox Moslem, observing all the practices of his creed. When he grew up he joined the army of Sonni Ali, king of Songhay. In time he rose to be a general, and finally, because of his great abilities, was made prime minister.

Sonni Ali, the sixteenth king of his dynasty, was one of the most renowned soldiers in African history. A ruthless conqueror and a stern ruler, he was subject to gusts of passion of which in his sober moments he repented. Between him and Mohammed Abu Bekr there developed one of those close and lasting friendships familiar to students of African biography. The prime minister saved his master from himself. Having no fear of Sonni Ali, he exercised a strong and healthy influence over the wild and despotic king.

When Sonni Ali became king, Timbuktu, having belonged to the rival kingdom of Melle, had passed into the hands of the Tuaregs, the strange veiled people of the desert. Sonni Ali resolved to take the town, with its seat on the

broad waters of the Niger. Having captured
the place, he proceeded to sack it without mercy;
no one but Mohammed Abu Bekr was able to
stay his hand. The king frequently decreed an
unjust execution of some subject of his. Mohammed Abu Bekr dared to conceal the culprit
until the royal wrath had cooled. Sometimes his
struggles with the king were long continued; in
such cases Mohammed's mother was wont to
help. She would let it be known in Timbuktu
that her son was withstanding Sonni Ali, that
the people might pray in the mosque for his
success.

Sonni Ali pushed his conquests both among
the neighboring Moslem kingdoms and in the
pagan belt, until at last his empire stretched inland (see map) from west to east some two
thousand miles from the Atlantic Ocean, and
was bounded on the south by the pagan lands
bordering the Gulf of Guinea, and on the north
by the slopes of the Atlas Mountains. In 1492
he was returning from a successful campaign
when he was drowned by the sudden flooding of
a stream. He left sons to succeed him. But,
supported by the good-will of the people, Mohammed Abu Bekr rose up against them, defeated them in battle, and seized the vacant

throne. It is said that when news of his doings was brought to Sonni Ali's daughters they cried, "Askia!" ("Usurper!") The epithet was calmly accepted by Mohammed as the title of his dynasty. He became the first and greatest Askia, and other Askias reigned over the Songhay empire until its final destruction by the Moors.

Chroniclers dwell mainly on the Askia's prowess as a soldier, but Barth, who spent some months in Timbuktu in the middle of the nineteenth century and made careful research into the records, points out that it is rather as a great civil administrator that he should be judged. Here his gifts were of no common order; he stands high in the long line of eminent Africans who have been competent men of affairs. The vast unwieldy areas of Sonni Ali's dominions, and those added by the Askia himself, he placed under known and trusty governors. Subject to their well regulated control, each area was allowed to retain its own form of local government. In order for his subjects to be released for peaceful pursuits, a standing army was substituted for general military service. It soon became evident that, great general though he was, the new ruler cared for industry and agriculture, and favored men of learning. He encouraged his people to give religion the place he gave it himself.

When he had spent three years adjusting the affairs of his vast dominions, Mohammed Abu Bekr committed his realm to the care of a well chosen regent and set off on a two-years' pilgrimage to Mecca. Mansa Musa, the great and good king of Melle, had made a like pilgrimage two hundred years before, traveling in pomp and magnificence with a great army and a long baggage train. The Askia took only a thousand footmen and five hundred horsemen as escort. His aim was to learn, rather than to impress other peoples with his greatness. At the time when Christopher Columbus was seeking the New World, this African ruler gathered around him men of learning and sanctity, and set out with them and his eldest son eastward to the Prophet's tomb.

The royal pilgrim noted everywhere the laws and customs which ministered to the welfare of the people. The riches which he brought back with him were the knowledge he had gained, and the friendship of many sages and scholars who remained his counsellors all through his long life. Bold though his acceptance of the title of usurper had been, Mohammed Abu Bekr evidently felt that, as he lacked the right of inheritance by birth, religious sanctions would set him more securely on his throne. So while he was in Cairo on his pilgrimage he resigned his possessions and dignities into the hands of the caliph of Egypt, remained without them for three days, and then received them back from the caliph in formal investiture.

On his return to the Sudan in 1497 the Askia, being then well over fifty years of age, set himself once more to administrative work. Besides the friends gained on his pilgrimage, he had round him a group of men whose minds had expanded with his own; foremost among them was Ali Foden, who became to Mohammed Askia what he himself had been to Sonni Ali.

At heart he was a man of peace. An old Arab writer says of him, "God made use of his service in order to save the true believers in Negroland from their sufferings and calamities." Yet he was incessantly driven to war with the pagan kingdom of Mossi; with the kingdom of Melle, which he finally subdued and settled; with the Fulani, with Borgu and with the Hausa states. In order to establish friendly relations, the conqueror frequently took to wife a woman of the

conquered race.[2] Four of Mohammed Askia's
sons succeeded him, and each was born of a
mother from a newly vanquished territory.

The social and administrative reforms insti-
tuted by this old-world African have a strangely
modern sound. His vast empire was held in con-
tentment and control. Barth, the German traveler before referred to, says, "He governed the
subject tribes with justice and equity, causing
well-being and comfort to spring up everywhere." He concerned himself with the principles of taxation, especially the land tax and the
tribute to be paid by conquered people; he developed trade, especially along the waterway of
the Niger; he introduced reforms in the markets,
and had weights and measures standardized and
inspected; he adjusted custom duties; he improved the system of banking and of credit; he
made laws for the suppression of immorality;
owing to the lax state of morals, he obliged
women to wear the veil in public; he is said
even to have tried to introduce better manners.

The Askia, who had been born and educated
on an island in the Niger, was able to maintain
friendship on equal terms with the most cultured men whom the civilization of Egypt had

[2] For another instance of this practice, see Mohlomi, p. 75.

produced. Learning flourished; large libraries were the cherished possession of the rich; the University of Sankore was thronged with students, and its teachers held intercourse with institutions of learning in other lands. Music was a joy to the people; chess-playing was a favorite pursuit. Yet all the time barbarous punishments were used without compunction, and there was much unbridled license in the large towns like Gao, Jenné and Timbuktu.

Mohammed Askia reigned for six and thirty years. In his old age he became blind; as is too common in African history, his sons brushed him aside. Like Moshesh of Basutoland, he had a sad and cheerless end. In 1528 his eldest son deposed him. At first he was left in one of his palaces in comfort and in peace. But three years later a nephew usurped the throne, and the once great Askia was banished to a comfortless island in the Niger. From thence the blind old conqueror made one more bid for life. His son Ismail came by night to visit him in secret. The story, as Lady Lugard tells it, is this:

"Ismail sat down before his father. The Askia, taking hold of his son's arm, said: 'Heavens! how can an arm like this allow mosquitoes to devour me, and frogs to leap upon me, when there is nothing which so revolts me?' Ismail was an upright but not brilliant representative of his father's stock. He replied with grief that he could do nothing. The Askia replied by telling him where there was a secret stock of money, who were the men whom he might trust, and how he was to come into touch with them. And, sitting in his miserable dungeon, in all the feebleness of blind old age, the still unconquered monarch planned and dictated a scheme by which his unworthy nephew was removed from the throne he had usurped, and Ismail was seated upon it in his place."

Restored to a place of honor in the palace, the great Askia lived on until 1538, being aged about a hundred when he died. In any century and in any empire the qualities and deeds of Mohammed Abu Bekr Et-Tourti would entitle him to be called "the Great." A few familiar dates will aid imagination to picture how remarkable this Central African ruler was in truth. He ascended the throne when Christopher Columbus was discovering America. He died when Henry VIII of England was still on the throne. He was gathered to his fathers fifty years before the defeat of the Spanish Armada, seventy years before the colony of Virginia was founded by British colonists, more than eighty years before the Pilgrim Fathers landed at Plymouth, and two hundred and fifty years before George Washington became first President of the United States.

III. OSAI TUTU KWAMINA: FROM KUMASI TO THE COAST

OSAI TUTU KWAMINA was the first king of Ashanti who received white envoys at his court and led his armies to the coast of the Gulf of Guinea. To find him at home we must span more than two centuries from the time of Mohammed Askia, and drop southward from Timbuktu seven hundred miles through the pagan country to the city of Kumasi.

In age, in size, in trade, in learning, Kumasi is not comparable with the past glory of Timbuktu. Nevertheless, set on its rocky hillside surrounded by forests, it is one of the African cities which has made a mark in history. It became the capital of Ashanti early in the eighteenth century, when Osai Tutu, the renowned ancestor after whom Tutu Kwamina was named, built up the power of the kingdom. He gave the people their most precious possession, the Golden Stool,[1] the center of all their history.

[1] The story is told and its significance interpreted in *The Golden Stool*, by Edwin W. Smith.

This first Tutu was a wise and able man. In his day justice was said to be ever on the alert; neither wealth nor office won favor in the judgments of the king or of his courts. He was a great fighter and was killed in battle. Four kings of his line succeeded him. Osai Tutu Kwamina was the fifth. He ascended the throne in 1800 and reigned for twenty-four years.

The origin of the Ashantis is uncertain; they, together with the Fantis and other coastal tribes, are probably part of the Akan people. They are fine in physique, cleanly in personal habits and in the sanitary arrangements of their towns, courageous and honorable, with a passionate love for their nation. Their system of customary law and social order is intricate and of great interest to the anthropologist. Before civilizing influences touched them they were ferocious in warfare, merciless to their captives, horribly cruel in their punishments, and wont to celebrate religious rites with an orgy of sacrifice, often of human beings. Their recorded doings are sometimes ruthless and barbaric to an incredible degree. Their friends found them a singularly attractive people; the hatred of their enemies knew no bounds.

Osai Tutu Kwamina had in heightened meas-

ure all the virtues of his people; he was also imbued with their faults. He differed from them
in having ability above the average, and a certain poise of mind and breadth of judgment bred
in him by the responsibilities of state.

The story of the Gold Coast, which lay between Ashanti, with its tributary kingdoms, and
the sea, is a stirring but in part a sordid history.
All along the coast there was a medley of black
and white. Lesser states, where tribes more or
less akin in race were at issues among themselves,
were making and dissolving alliances, now with
one another, now with the threatening Ashantis
in the rear. Among them was a fringe of forts
or trading lodges, some dating back five hundred
years, owned by Portuguese, Dutch, British,
Danish and Swedish traders and even by Bran-
denburgers from Prussia. The old maps of the
period show their names hanging from the coast-
line like leeches from the stem of a plant.

There is an uncertain record of French discovery and settlement in the fourteenth century.
Prince Henry the Navigator, son of John I of
Portugal, whose brilliant enterprise was arrested
by his death in 1463, probably did not pass beyond Sierra Leone. But he secured the first of
those Papal Bulls which conferred all rights in

the West Coast of Africa upon the Portuguese. In 1481-82 John II of Portugal sent a fleet to the Gold Coast with material ready prepared to build a fort and a church. The fleet anchored off Elmina, the Portuguese standard was hoisted on a tree, an altar was erected, mass was said for the conversion of the Africans. In twenty days, amid somewhat reluctant Natives, the fort had risen high enough to be capable of defense.

The Reformation in Europe put a new complexion on Papal Bulls. English and French privateers, no longer bound by the orders of the Pope, began to make trading trips along the coast. The adventurous captains divided their time between bartering stuffs—powder and muskets, or rum, for gold, ivory and slaves—and fighting the Portuguese or one another. In 1595 the Dutch began settlements which were the scenes of conflict with the Portuguese, each side enlisting Native allies. Gradually the Portuguese interest was diverted to the New World, and the Dutch and English got firmer hold on the Gold Coast and built more forts. The sites for these forts were not bought but rented. An agreement was embodied in a Note, and year by year the payment of the promised sum was recorded. These Notes changed hands as one tribe conquered another, and were a fruitful source of dissension between the traders and the Native peoples. In 1642, having been a hundred and sixty years in the country, Portugal ceded her settlements to Holland, receiving in return the interest of the latter country in Brazil.

But the darkest shadow is not yet in the picture; the iniquities and miseries of the slave trade surpass the warring of uncivilized tribes and the rivalries of trading nations. Portugal was foremost in the activity, serving as carrier for Spain, who, barred from direct access to the Gold Coast, was in desperate straits for labor in the West Indies, where the aboriginal Indians had been killed off by the reckless cruelties in the sugar plantations.

But Portugal did not stand alone. Most of the trading forts had slave rooms, where captives, sometimes up to a thousand in number, could be detained until they were shipped overseas. The English came into the trade in 1562, when Captain (afterwards Sir John) Hawkins took three cargoes of slaves to the West Indies. Queen Elizabeth demurred at first; afterwards she lent Hawkins a ship of her own, called the *Jesus,* and granted him as coat of arms a Negro laden with chains.

When Osai Tutu Kwamina became king in 1800, the slave traffic was still rife on the coast; the Abolition Act which made the deportation of slaves illegal was not passed till 1807, and at first did not operate effectively. As imagination pictures the situation created by rival traders, quarreling tribes, a shameless slave trade, and the ambitious Ashantis hovering in the background, the Gold Coast at the opening of the nineteenth century does not seem an attractive land. At this time Ashanti was already a considerable empire, neighboring kingdoms such as Denkera, Akim, Akwamu and Wassaw owing it allegiance. Each conquered state was put under a governor, who generally lived in Kumasi and went to his district only to collect tribute. Military service was also required, but rule was loose and provinces were frequently in rebellion.

The new king had plenty of work on hand. It was not till seven years had elapsed that the coast situation became unendurable. The Fantis, gathering round them a number of lesser tribes and states, had insulted and provoked their warlike inland enemies. A great Ashanti army was sent to the coast. Picturesquely enough, they at once sent the king some calabashes full of salt water. Then they got to work.

The battle of Anamabu, the chief Fanti town, ended in horrible slaughter. The wretched Fantis, who were poor fighters compared with their assailants, were driven into the sea, where those who escaped clung terror-stricken to rocks. Numbers of fugitives who had taken refuge in Cape Coast Castle were shamefully divided, by agreement between the conquerors, who sacrificed them, and the British governor himself, who sold most of his share as slaves.

The claim of the Ashantis that they were conquerors of the coastal tribes was admitted, but when the northern armies withdrew, the old tribal rivalries became active and the roads were closed to inland trade.

In 1811 the Ashantis again came south to chastise the Fantis; in 1814 there was once more open war. Trade could not prosper under these conditions. Some understanding with the Ashantis had to be sought. In 1817 the British Company trading on the Gold Coast sent up an embassy to Kumasi. After many negotiations with the king a treaty was drawn up and signed. White men have seldom had a less congenial task, for the king, as admitted conqueror, was entitled to receive rent for the trading forts, some of the Notes were actually in his possession, and

the record of payments was far from satisfactory
or clear. It is humiliating to find that in the
judgment of the best historians equity lay not
with the traders but with the king. His clear
memory, his shrewd questions, and his determi-
nation to get his rights were not easy to evade.

Peace did not last long. Two years later difficulties grew acute again. Coastal tribes insulted
the king's messengers; he held that the British
Company was pledged to get him redress. He
wanted to fine not only the offending Natives
but also the governor for his breach of faith.
Things were indeed threatening; the Company
began to strengthen their fortifications, which
further enraged the king. At this critical junc-
ture it was suggested that a man who had been
sent out as consul by the British government
might be able to intervene. He was on the coast
and eager to be of use. One king—especially if
he be an African—is always glad to deal with
another. The consul was invited to Kumasi,
representing not the Company but the English
king.

In Kumasi, confronted with charges of bad
faith, he was shown what was held to be a broken
treaty and Notes with payments in arrears. It
was not easy to explain why in one of the Notes

rum was charged at three times the Dutch traders' price. The consul did his best: had a new treaty drafted and signed; promised to get the earliest possible ratification of it; and left on such friendly terms that Osai Tutu Kwamina actually spat in his hand as he bade him good-by, a token of high honor. But unhappily there was strain between the consul and the governor at the coast. The treaty was ignored, the Ashanti ambassadors accompanying it were refused a passage; the discomfited consul hastened alone to England, imploring the Ashanti king to wait eight months for confirmation of the treaty he had signed. Ten months passed and Tutu Kwamina heard nothing. He began to concentrate his forces for war. The Ashantis transferred their trade from the British to the Dutch and the Danes.

In 1821 the British Parliament, believing that the slave trade was not being vigorously repressed nor the public money granted to the Company well expended, transferred the possessions on the Gold Coast to the Crown and placed them under the government of Sierra Leone.

This measure, which might have meant a happy settlement, led to acute conflict. The able and courageous Governor of Sierra Leone,

Sir Charles McCarthy, at first favorably dis-
posed towards Tutu Kwamina, was misled into
believing that he must crush the Ashanti power
before there could be peace. The coastal tribes
acclaimed his coming with enthusiasm. The
thing they most wanted was to have the Ashantis
crushed. Tutu Kwamina believed that once
again the treaty he had signed was being dishonored. A great Ashanti army moved southward
and met a small force under Sir Charles Mc-
Carthy, consisting mainly of allies from the
coastal tribes. They were easily overwhelmed.
Sir Charles McCarthy was killed; his head was
sent as a trophy to Kumasi, and his heart was
eaten by Ashanti leaders who admired his courage and wanted by this means to secure it for
themselves. The news came in a private letter
that on the day that Sir Charles McCarthy was
killed, Osai Tutu Kwamina died in Kumasi.

The further story of Ashanti wars passes out
of the range of this volume. But in Chapters
IX and X we shall revisit the Gold Coast as it
is today.

The embassies to Kumasi in 1817 and 1819
have enriched our libraries with two notable
quarto volumes, which transport us into the

presence of the king and his court.[2] The writer
of the first has an artistic eye for form and color,
a taste for the curious and the bizarre, and an
ear for music, some of which he transcribes.
The writer of the other depreciates Native archi-
tecture, is irritated by barbaric splendor, and
finds African music—of which he had to endure
a good deal—to be merely discordant noise. But
both are at one in their estimate of the king.

Bowdich thus describes the entry of the first
embassy into Kumasi. Upwards of five thousand people, mostly warriors, greet them with
awe-inspiring bursts of music; the air is full of
smoke from saluting muskets; flags—English,
Dutch and Danish—wave in confusion. The
embassy halts while war captains perform a wild
dance in the center of the circle. Progress is
as slow as in a thronged thoroughfare in New
York or London; streets branching to right or
left are crammed with heads. Through the
open house-fronts groups gaze on the first white
men. Another halt is made while chiefs
pass with their gorgeous trains. Bands of horns
and flutes play wild melodies; immense umbrellas of gay color, with valance or fringe,

---

[2] *Mission from Cape Town Castle to Ashanti*, by T. Edward Bowdich;
Murray, London, 1819. *Journal of a Residence in Ashanti*, by J. Dupuis;
Colburn, London, 1824.

crowned with gold models of elephants or peli-
cans or the crescent and other devices, shelter
groups from the burning sun and sway as their
bearers move; huge fans make small currents of
air in the stifling dust. A horrible spectacle
passes along the street—a man being cruelly tormented prior to being sacrificed.

In the market-place, nearly a mile in circum-
ference, the king stands in the distance, re-
splendent, surrounded by tributaries, captains,
and attendant warriors. More than a hundred
bands burst into music, each playing the special
air of its chief; horns sound defiance, drums are
beaten; then all is hushed except the soft breath-
ings of long flutes. Behind the great foreground
of the swaying umbrellas are the state ham-
mocks, covered with crimson taffeta and draped
in rich cloths. King's messengers with gold
breastplates clear the way, leading the white men
from chief to chief round the great assembly.

The flourish of horns grows more prolonged
and the drums louder. The embassy are passing
through the officers of the household of the king:
the chamberlain, the gold-horn blower, the captain of the messengers, the captain for royal exe-
cutions, the captain of the market, the keeper
of the royal burial ground, the master of the

band; the cook with a quantity of massive silver plate before him, the huge executioner with his stool clotted with blood and partly covered with fat; the king's four linguists encircled with splendor, their gold canes, tied in bundles like Roman fasces, held aloft; the keeper of the treasury with his boxes, scales, and weights of solid gold.

At last the king himself. One by one the embassy approach him—a man perhaps eight and thirty years of age, inclined to corpulence, full of dignity and composure, with handsome features, a shaven head and a short beard. "A mild and pleasing countenance, open, lively and animated, with a quick and penetrating eye." [3] His low chair is decked with gold; he wears a dark green silk cloth and sandals of soft white leather. From head to foot he is adorned with gold ornaments of delicate workmanship, and aggri beads and charms. On one hand a pair of small gold castanets on finger and thumb when clapped together secure silence. Elephants' tails spangled with gold are waved like a cloud before him.

The first of many interviews is over. It is eight o'clock on a lovely starlit night. Torches flash on the splendor of the king's regalia and

[3] *A Voyage to Africa*, by Hutton, 1820, p. 218.

throw in relief three skulls of his enemies which adorn the largest drum. Behind him follow aunts, sisters, and other women of his family, with rows of fine gold chains about their necks. The long retinue sweeps on after him, and the tired and amazed white men go to rest.

It is common, in African story, to find a man merciless in war, prodigal in human sacrifice, capricious and passionate, yet amiable, generous and of a benevolent turn of mind in ordinary life. The consistency of Tshaka, who shows no redeeming feature beyond attachment to his mother, is almost unmatched. Tutu Kwamina is described as candid, courteous, engaging, conciliatory, and wisely inquisitive. By shrewd questions he gets at the heart of things. The testimony to his honor never dims. One of the governors of Cape Coast Castle wrote of him in a despatch: "In all my negotiations with the king I had cause to remark what I have not experienced on the sea coast, the strictest regard to his word. In fact I look on the king as a high character. He is of middling stature, remarkably well-made, and of a handsome, open countenance." Consul Dupuis, on receiving the news of his death, characterized him thus: "The inflexible, the hospitable, the celebrated, the friendly, the distressed Osai Tutu Kwamina."

There are charming glimpses of the king among the children—another record typical of Africa. The children had their gayest time when he had leisure to play. They were not out of place at his knee during a business interview. He sent them to welcome the white men on arrival, and again to offer thanks for a present of sugar. The king said: "White men have good hearts, for they love little children." Young men he kept near him to be trained for leadership. He would give them a sum of gold and ask no questions for a year or more. Then he would call in his loan. The profit made on it would serve to pay the fee for promotion to higher dignity. If a man had wasted his money he lost his chance of promotion, yet the king was prepared himself to pay the fees for young and worthy captains if they were poor.

The chiefs and governors of the provinces exercised great power in council. Absolute monarch though he was, Tutu Kwamina could not always take his own way. "I must do what the old men say: I cannot help it," he sometimes remarked. There were violent scenes when the king was for peace and all his chiefs for war. He kept up a close system of espionage; there was little in his far-flung dominions which did not come to his ears. But if there was any cause for secrecy at Kumasi, he could put an oath on his people which no man dared to break.

Taxes were levied on slaves sent to the coast, on elephant hunting, on certain places where gold was found, on increase in a chief's gold ornaments, and on other things. Gold dropped in the market-place was the property of the king. In times of need the soil of the market-place was washed out and the gold used for national purposes. This was done twice in Tutu Kwamina's reign, with a yield to the value of several hundred pounds. During the visit of the embassy a man was beheaded for picking up some gold he had dropped in the market-place.

War, legislation and mechanical inventions were subjects on which the king liked to talk. He inquired much, as is usual in Africa, about his fellow-monarch in England, and proposed to send George IV a present of fifty beautiful boys and the same number of girls, all in rich dresses and gold. He could not understand why the slave trade had been stopped. He would give his brother of England ten thousand slaves if he would let it be resumed. He argued that Moslems, who had the same God as the Christians, came down to buy slaves and taught them good things. He explained that he did not go to hunt for slaves himself, he only went to war. When he killed a king, "then his gold, his slaves, his people are mine." When the king of Denkera failed to pay tribute as his father had done, it was natural to kill him and bring more than twenty thousand of his people to Kumasi. The bad ones were killed and Tutu's stool was washed with their blood. The good ones became slaves and were sold or given to his captains. White kings had themselves bought slaves on the Gold Coast. Why could not the trade go on?

Tutu Kwamina certainly gloried in his wars. At times the linguists or spokesmen publicly recited his doings. Then his eyes sparkled with animation, the audience began to hum war songs, the king moved his body and feet in cadence with the verse. Then he broke out into revilings of his former enemies, and perhaps had some imprisoned prince brought before him that he might glory over his lost estate.

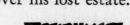

IV. A NIGERIAN ROMANCE: THE CAREER OF BISHOP CROWTHER

IN the middle of the nineteenth century an African clergyman, wise and kindly of face, gentle and unobtrusive of bearing, was a familiar figure in missionary circles in Britain. His name was Samuel Adjai Crowther. Dr. Eugene Stock, the historian of the Church Missionary Society, says that his was one of the most remarkable careers in the whole history of the church of Christ. Who was this man? Two incidents during this visit of his to London stimulate curiosity and make inquiry seem worth while.

One day Crowther sat in a mission house in London busy at some work of translation. An Englishman, evidently a man of standing, entered the room on some business of his own. The translator looked up, gave a cry of pleasure, threw his pen aside, and ran to embrace the astonished newcomer, making eager references to a former meeting. The quick and retentive African memory had bridged the gulf of thirty years. Sir Henry Leeke, now a retired admiral of the British Navy, recalled the circumstances at once, returned hearty greetings, and invited his African friend to stay at his country house and preach in the village church.

About the same time Queen Victoria, the Prince Consort, and Lord Wriothesley Russell bent heads with this same African over a map, discussing West African affairs. Not at first did the African realize that the gracious lady who for half an hour talked so freely and kindly with him was the British Queen. Why was Samuel Adjai Crowther brought to see Queen Victoria? What were they all studying on the map?

In the town of Oshogun in the Yoruba country a happy family, like hundreds of others each in their own brown hut, were enjoying their breakfast on a lovely summer morning in the year 1821. Suddenly a wild alarm—the slave raiders were upon them, near at hand. The father fled to join those manning the weak mud walls of the town. The mother made ready to escape with her children to the bush. But it was too late; the slavers had made good their entrance, burning and slaying as they came. The father of the happy family was heard of no more; the mother and children were captured and driven off to be sold.

The eldest boy Adjai in later years wrote the story of what he thought and felt. This record of an African boy's reaction to calamity is probably unique in its detail of woe. Separated from his mother and the younger children, he was swept out into a loneliness peopled by dreadful fears. Eagerly on the long slave march he scanned each landmark, that he might find his way home if he should be able to escape; sadly his ears noted the change from one dialect to another; hope grew faint when he heard the fourth strange tongue. He was bartered for a horse, for rum, for tobacco; he became "a veteran in slavery"; misery led him to try to take his life. His worst secret terror came slowly, but at last it came. He saw the first white man —a Portuguese slaver—and trembled at the touch of a strange white hand.

The boy was a good bit of human merchandise; the Portuguese bought him and took him to the coast. Stiff with fright he was sent in a canoe across the Lagos River, an awful stretch of water which seemed to sever him finally from home. The slave-ship stood in the offing; the slaves were shipped in the dark from Lagos beach. Stowed in the hold in misery and hunger, they passed a wretched night.

Next morning the scene had changed. The hatches were opened; the Portuguese sailors stood bound and sullen; the slaves were set free. All round them were British sailors; a savory smell of breakfast was in the air. The slave-trading vessel had been caught as she was trying to slip away with her living cargo. The rescued Africans, who could neither be taken back to their homes nor landed where they would only be recaptured, were sent round the West African coast in the British vessels to the settlement for freed slaves at Sierra Leone. Adjai and some other boys were put on board H.M.S. *Myrmidon;* the sailors made pets of them; the captain became their friend. It was this captain whom Crowther recognized thirty years later in London as the man who had rescued him from misery and opened his door to life.

Adjai went to a mission school in Sierra Leone and learned quickly. In his own home the boys had been bred to activity and independence. He had raised chickens and farmed a small bit of land successfully before the slave-raiders came. Now he turned his energies to his books. By December 1825 he had become a Christian, and was baptized as Samuel Adjai Crowther.

Adjai was taken to London while still a lad by

two of his missionary teachers, and for eight months attended an ordinary parochial school. It was probably a dreary experience for a young African, but it laid the foundation of the excellent English which he afterwards spoke.

Returning to Sierra Leone, he entered as first student at the newly opened Fourah Bay College. On leaving it as a trained teacher he was appointed to a little school. He married a girl who had been rescued like himself. In the early days they had done their lessons together. She was baptized and, like him, called after some worthy English friend, exchanging her pretty African name Asano for that of Susan Thompson. They had three sons and three daughters and lived happily together for fifty years.

Crowther was about to enter a new field of romance. The minds of men who cared for Africa were turning to the Niger; not those great stretches on either side of Timbuktu, but the long reaches of the lower waters, almost unknown, and the Benue River flowing into the Niger at Lokoja from the east, and wholly unexplored. Influential men after more than thirty years of effort were convinced that the slave trade could not be stopped by capturing slave ships at sea. The areas living on the sale of slaves must be given some more profitable trade. This was afterwards David Livingstone's persistent plea. Treaties made with chiefs along the river banks might check the trade at its source; if trade with the Niger territory could once be opened, humanity would triumph and commerce increase.

The British government in 1841 agreed to equip and send out an expedition; the Church Missionary Society had permission to send with it two men. They chose a missionary of German origin, with a gift for the acquisition of African tongues, and also Samuel Adjai Crowther, whose intelligence and capacity already marked him out as a pioneer. The expedition was derided before it started—in those days enough was not known of Africa to make it seem worth while to face risks; it was still more derided when the few broken fragments returned. Out of one hundred and fifty Europeans forty-two died within two months. The three vessels, having pushed slowly up the river, returned one by one with invalided men.

In the eyes of white men the expedition spelled disastrous failure; to Crowther limitless opportunities opened out. He went to and fro among chiefs and villagers; men, women and children, Moslem and pagan, became his friends. His published journal, for all its set and old-fashioned phrases, is full of freshness and life. As the white men sickened he tended them; as they died he laid them in their lonely graves. And there was born in him a sense that notwithstanding their courage and devotion, it was not by them but by Africans that God's harvest on the Niger would be sown and reaped.

The next stage of eventful life was not on the Niger, but in the Yoruba country whence Crowther himself had come. His pioneering gifts claimed further training and wider use. For the second time he went to England, studied in a theological college, passed his ordination examination creditably, and was ordained a clergyman of the Church of England—the first African clergyman on the Church Missionary Society's roll.

He was chosen to go with a small party to minister to a new settlement in the Yoruba country, consisting partly of remnants of the Egba tribe left by slave-raiders, and partly of some Egba traders who had been carried off as slaves, rescued, and taken to Freetown. Later they had returned to their original district and settled round a great rock, naming their new town Abeokuta, or Under-Stone. The Egbas from Sierra Leone were Christian, at least in name; they asked for teachers for themselves and for the heathen in the town.

On his way from England to Abeokuta Crowther stopped at Sierra Leone. "The black man who was crowned a minister" received a welcome as warm as that given to Dr. Aggrey at the Gold Coast (see p. 132). He, too, had spent his boyhood in their midst. Crowds flocked to hear him as he preached in English or in his own Yoruban tongue. He went and sat down among fanatical Shango worshippers; he reasoned with them and they heard. The Mohammedans respected him.

The road to Abeokuta was closed by war until 1846. Then the party entered the town and received a splendid welcome from Chief Sagbua. Land and money were given to build a church.

One day a rumor reached Crowther's ears that the mother from whose side he had been torn in the slave raid was alive and not far off. The rumor proved true. The old mother received back her long-lost son. "When she saw me," wrote Crowther in his journal, "she trembled, she could not believe her own eyes. We grasped one another in silence and great astonishment.

Big tears rolled down her emaciated cheeks. She held me by the hand and called me by the familiar names I used to be called by my grandmother. We could not say much, but sat casting many an affectionate look at one another. I had given up all hope and now, after a separation of twenty-five years, we were brought together again." The old mother Afala stayed gladly with her new-found son. She became the first convert in the Abeokuta mission.

The Christian community in Abeokuta grew strong, and bore with fortitude the persecution which came upon it. In 1851 Kosoko, king of Lagos, and Gezo, king of Dahomey, came up with a great army against the town. A terrible battle was fought, the Christians aiding in the defence of the walls. The foe was defeated and driven off. Crowther was appalled to find dead on the battlefield numbers of women, the renowned Amazons of Dahomey.

For the third time Crowther revisited England and paid his visit to the Queen. The African clergyman was competent to inform the Queen and her ministers about his country's affairs. He could tell of the slave trade still lurking in the lagoons, of the fierce attack of the kings upon Abeokuta, of the faithfulness of the Christians there. He had sound views on political and commercial questions.

Again the scene of Crowther's life was changed. Instead of carrying on at Abeokuta he was sent with the second Niger expedition in 1854. This was entirely successful; there was no serious illness or loss of life; valuable treaties were made with the tribes; chiefs and people were ready to be friends. The leader credited Crowther with much of the success. He, on his part, was convinced more firmly than ever that the time had come for Africans to evangelize the riverine tribes. In 1857 a third expedition went up the river and with it Crowther again. He was now head of a mission party to be planted out along the banks. Misadventures were many, but the work took root. Year by year groups of Christians formed themselves in isolated places into the beginnings of a church. Christian Africans brought as teachers from Sierra Leone were waiting to be ordained pastors. The mission needed a bishop, but what white man, as things then were on the Niger, could go up and down the river to do a bishop's work?

Crowther was again in England in 1864. The great missionary statesman Henry Venn, head of the Church Missionary Society, had long cherished a plan which was now given effect. The Niger mission should be entirely manned by Africans: it should have an African bishop, and Samuel Adjai Crowther was the man.

The proposal was startling but it gained support. Obstacles and difficulties melted away. Crowther's own reluctance was overcome by the confident faith of Henry Venn. The consecration, in the midst of a multitude of praying people, took place in Canterbury Cathedral in June 1864. Sir Henry Leeke of H.M.S. *Myrmidon* was there, and a venerable missionary widow who had taught the Black Bishop his alphabet when he was rescued from slavery and brought to Sierra Leone.

The story of Bishop Crowther's long episcopate, covering seven and twenty years, has never yet been studied in the fuller light of the missionary experience of today. With blameless character and unsparing devotion the chief pastor moved among his scattered flock, preaching his message, reaching out to the heathen round. With Lagos as his center he went up and down the river, when means of communication offered; year by year his simple reports told of progress. Down in the noisome parts of the Niger delta the gospel did its cleansing work.

In Bonny the sacred iguanas, huge repulsive lizards, ceased to lord it in the streets; in Brass snake worship was forsaken. Fires of persecution burned, but the flame fed the church.

Yet all was not well on the Niger. Some of the mission agents fell into sin; others grew lax and cold. Polygamy laid its hand upon the church. The bishop, himself a saint, was slow to perceive evil, too gentle to cut it out. The committee at home, though their trust in him never faltered, were ill at ease. A helper or two went from England to reinforce his staff; a steamer was sent to make supervision possible even when the river was low; a conference was held at Madeira to lay plans with the bishop for reform. But still unsatisfactory reports kept coming. At last the details of a horrible murder at Onitsha, in which professing Christians were concerned, raised a storm in the public press. A party of British missionaries who went to open up work in the Sudan with Lokoja as their base made grave representations as to the low level of Christian life in the Niger church; the committee in London felt that disciplinary action must be taken. The bishop prepared loyally to co-operate with them, though he felt that to some of his African colleagues injustice was being done. Under the strain of this deep distress his health gave way. He died on the last day of 1891.

Dr. Eugene Stock wrote, with intimate knowledge of Crowther and of his career:

"Amid circumstances of almost unexampled difficulty, and in face of discouragements and disappointments innumerable, he went steadily on his way with indomitable perseverance in a holy cause. . . . He lived in an atmosphere of suspicion and scandal, yet no tongue, however malicious, of black man or white man, ventured to whisper reproach against his personal reputation. If it must be allowed that he was an Eli in exercising discipline too lightly, he was an Eli, too, in simplicity and sincerity of character."

There are no questions in the whole science of missions more germane to the present situation in Africa than those which arise out of this appointment of Samuel Crowther to be the first of a line of bishops of African race.

No one who reads this book will deny that other Africans, Christian and non-Christian, have shown broad administrative capacity and skill in dealing with men. Nor can there be question of the goodness and fidelity to duty shown by Crowther himself. But disaster always follows when "diversity of gifts" is not recognized. A man, whether white or black, may be a fearless pioneer, a stirring evangelist, even a gentle pastor, and yet come short in administrative and supervisory work.

Further, some sixty years ago the influence of heredity and environment, for good or evil, was given little weight. Crowther as a boy was cut off from the salutary aspects of tribal life, which at their best develop leadership and train in administrative work. He passed through one mission school after another, among youths detribalized like himself. His pure and gentle spirit met no blast of the forces of evil which co-exist with the good in tribal life; he had no personal experience of the deadly hold of sin upon the man who hesitates in face of them and yields. He went out to face the darkness of heathen strongholds, to preach the doctrines of sin and grace, to live a humble, blameless Christian life; but of passions of the human heart he was unaware. Can such a man discern secret evil or deal with it when found? To send an Anglo-Saxon man of Crowther's temperament and experience to lead the Niger mission, as things then were, would have meant unwisdom rather than faith.

Crowther's mission agents from Sierra Leone were under the same disabilities as himself; the force of superstition and pagan environment did not touch them till they stood as young men alone in its midst. And within many of them, unlike Crowther, was a human nature strong in primitive passions, ready to betray them to the tempters around. Sometimes the mission school measure of grace and discipline failed to meet their need. One can picture the good bishop visiting such men as a spiritual father and leaving their depths untouched.

It is probable, were the evidence thoroughly examined, that the failure in the Niger mission would reflect as much on the white man's wisdom as on the African's moral strength. Be that as it may, things go well on the Niger today. White and black work together in building a living church. And Samuel Adjai Crowther, first bishop and founder of the work, an example of godly life, is kept in constant and grateful remembrance.

V. TSHAKA THE ZULU: A BLACK NAPOLEON

PASSING from West to South Africa, we find ourselves in the midst of historical situations full of color and significance. Without some survey of the racial movements in the southern part of the continent there can be no intelligent and sympathetic study of the sons of Africa who there move across the stage of life. Tshaka (born about 1786, died 1828) comes into the middle of the scene. Moshesh follows, from the close of the eighteenth century to 1870.

In Stow's volume, *Native Races in South Africa,* there is an impressive map which shows the main lines of migration from times where the only guide is tradition, down to recent years. Broad streaks of color begin far north in the region of the great lakes and show the migrating races as they come from the center of the continent. These human rivers strike westward and southward until, toward the narrowing south, they mingle as in a whirlpool of waters. Still restlessly moving, as the dated entries show, they then turn northward towards the place whence

they came. The map is full of passionate confusion, with tribal masses here spreading out,
there forced together again.

The earliest migrants were the Bushmen, small
primitive hunters with bows and poisoned ar-
rows. Their broad course can be traced on the
eastern side of the continent by rock sculptures,
on the western side by vivid lifelike paintings,
often set in caves. Despised and hunted like
beasts by the other tribes, the Bushmen had
strange gleams of a higher past and of a northern
culture. There were many of these wild hunters
in South Africa when the first white men came.

Following the Bushmen and long after them
came the hordes of the Hottentots. They over-
ran their predecessors, seeking the richest pasture
westward and southward for their flocks.
When the white men found the Cape, Hottentots were there already, still at enmity with the
Bushman and trying to kill him out.

Behind the Hottentots came vast migrations
of the Bantu, dividing into two groups. Tribes
with the prefix Ba to their names spread far to
the west into the Congo basin and southward
through the central plains—the Bechuana and
Basuto among the rest. Tribes with the prefix
Ama—fierce warriors like the Ama-Xosa and

Ama-Zulu—passed down the eastern side. These tribes divided into many others, who were swept up against each other in the whirlpool and fought with desperation, as we shall see. On the map of migrations there are lines like a great fan, opening northward, to show the rise and spread of the dread Matebele power. And there are lines which curl northward like a ribbon to the Victoria Nyanza and then turn southward, to show the track of Sebituane, father of Mamochisane (see p. 223) who built up the great central Makololo power. A body of fighting Zulus, breaking out of the whirlpool, sought room elsewhere and became the Angoni tribe. And there is a sweeping circle to show how the Mantatis went blindly round and round in their raids. The tribal movements twist and twirl as if frenzied terror and rage had blinded men.

Stow's map shows, too, by long black lines distinguished by dots and crosses, how white men from various lands came to the south as we have seen them come to the west. The first adventurers were the Portuguese. In 1487, again ten years later, and several times in the early years of the sixteenth century, they came and went. On the eastern coast they made settlements and pressed inland, but quite to the south the Portuguese made no mark.

Dutch and English sailing vessels came later, seeking fresh provisions on the long journey to or from India, and trading for cattle with the few Hottentots on the coast. In 1647 some shipwrecked Dutch sailors were stranded for a winter at the Cape. On their return to the Netherlands the Dutch East India Company resolved to open a refreshment station for passing ships at Table Bay, with a garden and hospital. Soon a few farmers, Dutch and French, began to come. The Hottentots and the farmers, good friends at first, disagreed and fought. The little settlement grew slowly. After fifty years there were about fourteen hundred white people in South Africa, including women and children. Cape Town had about eighty private houses. No white man lived more than forty-five miles from the Cape. The colonists had heard of the Orange River, but no white man had even set foot on the Karoo.

The Dutch farmers were full of enterprise. The next fifty years saw the small white stream flow onward till it met the edge of the great black stream surging south. There followed clash after clash with the Ama-Xosa, the first great Bantu race with whom the Dutch came face to face. An attempt was made to fix the Fish River as the boundary between the races, but boundaries had never meant much to the Ama-Xosa when cattle or anything they wanted lay on the other side.

Between the years 1781 and 1813, owing to wars in Europe, the Cape passed from the hands of the Dutch to the British and back again to the Dutch. Then it became part of the British Empire and has so remained, first as a colony, then as part of a great self-governing Dominion.

Fresh racial complications now began. The Dutch colonists were not happy under British rule. Many more British came. Both races wanted to use the language, the laws, the coinage, of the land from which they came. The two nations liked to govern, each in its own way. They differed especially as to the best way to treat with African tribes. The large number of slaves, who had been imported when Hottentot labor ran short, were set free by government ordinance in 1834 as part of the general movement for emancipation. This created bitter feeling, especially in regard to the compensation offered to the owners. At last the Dutch farm-

ers felt the time had come to move. They believed there was a vast wilderness northward
where the tribes had been destroyed by war.
There they would go with their families and
cattle and make for themselves new homes where
they would be free. So the long line of white
wagons and horsemen and cattle trekked into the
unknown northern land.

These *voortrekkers* of 1836 were stern and
courageous. They bent neither to friend nor to
foe. The country to which they went had indeed lost many of its old inhabitants, but it was
full of roving warriors as fearless as the emigrant
farmers themselves. The stories of that trek
thrill with their bravery and appal with their
destruction of life. The white men did not attack except when they felt it needful to punish,
but when attacked they fought with ruthless
skill. Laagers surrounded by masses of Zulu and
Matebele, ambushes and night alarms, daring
escapes and savage revenges, deadly gunfire and
stabbing assegai, gained victory now for the
white men, now for the black. That is the story
of the trek. The white stream pressed on, and
always the tribes struggled for supremacy
among themselves, or strove to hold the land
against the white invaders. This, in brief and

broken outline, is the background of history in front of which the chiefs of South Africa stand.

Among the migratory tribes were the Ama-Zulu, who settled in what afterwards became Natal. They were not a people of note. The chief of the Mtetwa was their feudal lord. To the reigning chief, Senzangakona, there was born a son in 1786. His mother, Nandi, took him, as was the Zulu custom, to her parents' house to be weaned when he was one year old. There he grew into a wild and restless lad, at issue with the world. He cared for no one but his mother; his relatives had no use for him.

When he was old enough to leave childhood behind, his father came to see him, bringing the loin-covering which was worn by elder boys and men. But Tshaka not only refused to receive it, he behaved so badly to his father that he had to flee from the tribe. His mother, Senzangakona's favorite wife, had high connections; she got her father to try what he could do with the boy. She left home and husband and went with her wayward son. But he soon got to the end of his grandfather's patience and was adrift in the world again.

At last Tshaka found a man who understood him and whom he was willing to obey. The young chief of the Mtetwa tribe, Dingiswayo, had himself known what it was to be a wanderer from home. He saw the capacity of the lad. He gave him asylum and made him a soldier in his army. Tshaka rose rapidly in his regiment and became Dingiswayo's friend. The two men fought together in the wars. Tshaka was now a favorite with the people. He had lived through his restless phase.

In the course of the years his father died and he became chief of the Zulu tribe, still keeping close to his Mtetwa friend. About the year 1812 Dingiswayo was captured in battle and afterwards put to death. Then the large Mtetwa tribe chose Tshaka, whom they knew as a leader of their armies, to be their chief, cast in their lot with his tribe, and took the name of Zulus.

Even today, when their glory as a ruling race has departed, the Zulus with their splendid and dignified bearing stand out among African races. Tshaka, at twenty-four years of age, in person excelled them all. He was notable for stature, agility and strength. He could do all the things which the tribe admired. His physical endurance never flagged. Not only was he a fearless warrior but he could sing and jest and dance with the rest. And to Tshaka dancing was no light relaxation but sustained and strenuous exercise.

A peaceful career was not open to Tshaka, nor to the chief of any pastoral tribe in his day. The choice lay between attacking and being attacked. To fight put no strain on his desires; his whole being was concentrated on war. Except that he honored and loved his mother, who loved him only and lived for her son, Tshaka's record shows no trace of tenderness for child or woman, no amiable weakness, no trace of penitence for misdeeds. His sternness was tempered by no mercy; his cruelty had no compunction or restraint. His supreme organizing ability; his rigid discipline of others and, in certain respects, of himself; his dauntless and resourceful courage; his amazing power of dominating, combining and using men, win a half-reluctant admiration. Those who shudder at his butcheries and massacres are constrained to admit the qualities of greatness in him. As long as history continues to put the soldier and the conqueror in the forefront of national heroes, Tshaka holds the right to a niche in the African temple of fame.

Dingiswayo had learned from some white men met in his early wanderings when he, like Tshaka, was away from his father's kraal, how

armies in Europe were drilled.   Hitherto in
tribal warfare warriors had followed their chief
en masse into battle, or out of it if defeat came.
Tshaka shared all that Dingiswayo knew.   But
he went far beyond.   The Zulu armies became
the wonder of the world.

Tshaka divided his soldiers into regiments,
grouping men near in age.   They lived under
close restraint; only a few had wives of their
own.   Even food was chosen with a view to fitting men for war.   The ranks were swelled by
choice youths captured in war time, who were
offered a choice between soldiering or slavery.
The old ungainly assegai was modified into a
short, deadly, cutting and stabbing weapon;
each soldier was sheltered behind a great shield
of cowhide, of varied color and pattern, which
hid his whole body.   The armies were trained to
fight in crescent shape: the main body, with re-
inforcements behind it, were in the center, two
long arms curving out and forward on either
side.   The deadly closing in of the Zulu "horns"
added a new terror to war.

The Zulus fought like demons, not only because they were brave and all their ideals were
of conquest, but because they knew that falter-
ing or failure led inexorably to death when they

stood before Tshaka on their return. Of the dread armies which he had fashioned Tshaka made full use. He spread terror far and wide, sweeping great regions bare of inhabitants; he ravaged the whole of Natal and went farther afield. He painted most of the lines and colors on Stow's map of migrations; the Matebele and Makololo peoples sprang up as the result of his doings, the fierce Angoni of Nyasaland took origin in a fragment severed from his hosts.

Tshaka at home was a replica of Tshaka at war. He was merciless in his punishments, which fell on men for no apparent cause. No life was safe. Executioners stood ready at a moment's notice to seize those who displeased the tyrant, and impale them on stakes in the forest for hyenas and other wild animals to eat. No courtier dared stand erect in his presence. Yet Tshaka called out lasting devotion. Dr. J. Dexter Taylor heard of an old Zulu servant who had been in charge of Tshaka's pet monkey, removing it from his side when the chief tired of playing with it. One day he inadvertently touched the skin of Tshaka's arm and felt a great thrill go through him. A missionary spoke to this old Zulu of heaven. He listened, then he asked if Tshaka would be there. The missionary hesitated. The old Zulu immediately declared he would rather serve his old chief in the other place than be in heaven separated from him.

Tshaka's mother, Nandi, pleaded with him to take a legal wife that the great dynasty might have an heir. But though hundreds of women belonged to Tshaka he gave none the place of wife. No children of his were allowed to live; either the mothers were put to death before childbirth or the baby was destroyed at once. The love of children, so marked among Africans, had no place in the iron personality of this Zulu chief. He ruled entirely by fear; the people, while they adored him, half hated him. At last his cruelties sickened them and the end of his power drew near.

In Tshaka's days the white men had not yet, for the most part, come into close contact with the strong Bantu tribes. A few white traders made their way to Tshaka's kraals. No missionaries entered his dominions, though several were at work to the south. His life ended thirteen years before Livingstone arrived in Africa. Tshaka twice sent messengers to Cape Town to make friends with the government there, and an official envoy was being despatched from Cape

Colony to discuss affairs with the chief at the time of his death.

To Africa itself Tshaka owes the best and the worst of what he was. He has been compared to Nero for his cruelty; he has been called the Black Napoleon because of his genius for war. Both titles half fit the man. His death in September 1828 was in this wise:

His armies had been defeated in battle, an unusual experience for them. Hunger had been rife, for the Zulus lived mainly on the spoils of war. The people had grown weary of bloodshed. The reaction against the tyrant had begun. Tshaka had seen to it that no son could usurp his place, but he had brothers, and from them came the assault. As he sat one evening before nightfall, talking with some chiefs and watching the cattle being driven into the kraal, two of his half-brothers crept up behind and stabbed him in the back. Mbopa, one of his favorite servants, came to help them. In a few minutes Tshaka was dead.

Tshaka, and still more Dingaan, the half-brother who succeeded him as chief, made the Zulus a name of dread. Old fears and antipathies die hard. But there is another side to the Zulu. Of the Africans present at that conference in Belgium where the discovery of the sons of Africa was made, there was one man, especially gentle, especially strong, and especially rich in wisdom and in spiritual fellowship. In South Africa he was a leader among his own people in Christian service and worship, and in social and political affairs. In England, where he came later, he was an honored guest, unassuming, mature in thought, sane in outlook, ready to give and to receive. This man was a Zulu.

VI. MOSHESH THE NATION-BUILDER

IN the regions affected by Tshaka's wars conditions were not propitious for nation-building. The Bantu tribes were broken and harried. Few of them had any stable base. Masses of fighting men, with their impedimenta of women, children and cattle, kept branching off under new leaders. Great fighters were flung up out of the whirlpool. Sebituane, chief of the newly formed tribe of the Makololo, with superb daring carved his way northward to the Zambezi, where Livingstone afterwards became his guest and friend; Umziligazi (Moselekatse) broke away from Tshaka, welded those who followed him into the dreaded Matebele and led them from victory to victory; Sekonyela, son of Ma-Ntatisi, the woman leader of the Mantatis (see p. 222), made the Batlakoa a disturbing factor for years.

But of all the Bantu leaders who rose before Tshaka's blood-red sun had set, the greatest was Moshesh, the founder of the Basuto nation. He built up his little mountain state in the midst

of warring Bantu rivals, while parties of white
and half-white adventurers, whose respect for
property was small, were surging to and fro;
and he accomplished his task on the debatable
ground where Briton and Boer met one another,
and boundaries between the old colony, the new
republics, and tribal territory were ill-defined.
The steep gulleys which alone gave access to
Moshesh's stronghold of Thaba Bosiu were not
more difficult to tread than were the thorny
paths of diplomacy through which he had to
pick his way.

Moshesh stands midway, in time and in enlightenment, between Tshaka, who scarcely
knew of the restraining influences of civilized
society, and Khama, chief of the Bamangwato,
who took into the heart of his African heritage
the Christian treasures of liberty, purity and
truth. Moshesh, like King Agrippa, was almost
but not quite persuaded to be a Christian. Unlike Lewanika of the Barotse, who withstood
the pleadings of François Coillard to the last,
Moshesh was baptized, but only at the very end
of his days. He stands at the parting of the
ways, between the old and new day in South
Africa, a figure of singular significance and in-

terest, one of the most attractive of South African chiefs.

He was born towards the close of the eighteenth century, about the time when Tutu Kwamina began to reign in Ashanti, by the Thlotsi River in the north of what is now Basutoland. His grandfather was a man of small account, named Peete. His father, Mokachane, a hunter and chief of a small village, was rather a character, reappearing at intervals in the story of his son's life. He was a dry old man, abrupt in speech, who cared little for white men; sugar was, in his opinion, the best thing they had brought to South Africa.

Moshesh grew up like other village boys. But one strong formative influence came into his life. He had a cousin named Mohlomi, then growing old, who was sought after and venerated for his wisdom. The stories of him suggest that in his animistic creed he had discerned the elements of the divine. Dr. Aggrey's account of the attitude of his father while his father was still a pagan always brought the South African sage to mind. Mohlomi claimed to have communion with God; he ate little and took no strong drink; he had a gift of healing and could work many cures. But he turned aside from divination and never "threw the bones." He read the hearts of men.

In an age when each man feared his fellow, Mohlomi would travel everywhere, passing from tribe to tribe. He believed in peace and in inter-tribal fellowship. Some of his ways of establishing it were strange. From each tribe visited he chose a wife, provided a house for her, and left her among her people. The child thus born was a link between him and the tribe and ensured a welcome for him on his return. So close did he come to the life of his neighbors that finding in one place a tribe whose wealth was in dogs, he stayed until he had earned enough dogs to pay in the current coin of the tribe the dowry of the woman he chose. He married her and went on his way.

Twice Moshesh had interviews with this sage. Mohlomi discerned his promise while he was still a lad and foretold his power. "My son," he said, "if thou wouldst forsake all, I would take thee with me whithersoever I go; but it may not be. One day thou shalt rule men. Learn then to know them. And when thou judgest, let thy judgments be just."

In his father's village Moshesh followed this advice. He frequented the *lekhotla*, or court,

where village business was done and where passing strangers came. He sought to know men.
The men of the village learned to listen when he
spoke. In due time he married, and then, according to common custom, he left his father's
village when he was about twenty years of age
and sought a place of his own. He chose Butha-
Buthe where his wife's relations lived.

The African has an unerring eye for character. Men rallied round Moshesh, hailing him
as leader and chief. First they came in ones and
twos, then in larger groups. Then a dispossessed chief brought in the last small remnant
of his tribe. Among these waifs and strays torn
from their tribal anchorage even Zulus came. It
was a strange medley of men differing in custom
and habit as well as in language, some being even
hereditary foes. But Moshesh cast out no one
who sought his protection, and set himself by
steady care and ceaseless discipline to weld his
fragments into a whole. He did it, too, for the
Basuto attained to nationhood and strenuously
cling to their nationhood still.

On one point Moshesh failed. He could not
restrain them from making forays or from taking revenge on their foes. As he sadly confessed
long years after in a letter to a high commis-

sioner, "The law of retaliation is at the bottom of our manners." Yet he was singularly free from revengeful desire himself. He would fain have lived in peace, but wandering forces under aggressive leaders thrust war on him again and again. The tangled stories of these assaults can be read in the many-volumed histories of South Africa by Cory and Theal, or in Sir Godfrey Lagden's volume, *The Basutos*. But such wars do not concern us except in so far as they bring out the qualities of the mountain chief.

The first great assault was made on Butha-Buthe by Sekonyela and the Batlakoa. They drove Moshesh into his stronghold and cut off his supplies; his cattle were captured and his crops destroyed. It became clear that Butha-Buthe was not secure enough for permanent settlement. The little growing nation must be moved. Moshesh heard of a less pregnable mountain fastness some twenty miles to the south. But how would a besieged chief break through the ring of an encircling army and transport women, children and cattle across open ground beset with perils and foes? There were not far off some bands of Umsiligazi's warriors seeking for prey. To them Moshesh sent a secret messenger to say that the Batlakoa, with great herds of cattle, were besieging him. The Mate-bele readily fell upon them and broke up the host. The way was now open for Moshesh to move to Thaba Bosiu, the Mountain of Night, a rocky stronghold which has ever since been the center of Basuto life.

On the way a kind of tragedy occurred which illustrates the resourceful humor of the chief. Misery and poverty had driven some wretched people to cannibalism. As Moshesh passed from Butha-Buthe, his grandfather Peete got sepa-rated from the host, was captured by a party of cannibals, and eaten, of course. Years after when Moshesh's eldest son Letsie was about to enter the initiation school a difficulty arose. The purification of his ancestors' graves was necessary before admission. His father and grandfather were living, but what about his great-grandfather's grave? The cannibal group who had caught and eaten old Peete were brought before Moshesh and he was urged to kill them. But Moshesh never killed a man if it could be avoided. "It is not becoming to disturb the graves of your ancestors," he calmly said. So the ceremony for the purification of graves was performed upon the cannibals. And Letsie was admitted to the initiation school.

It is interesting to find that while Khama a few years later steadily opposed them, Moshesh attached a real value to these initiation schools and supervised them himself. One year, when he had to be absent while the school was going on, he invited his former enemy Sekonyela, whom he was willing to treat as a friend, to come and supervise the school for him. It gave the Batlakoa chief the entry into Thaba Bosiu, which he would never have won for himself. He shamefully abused the trust. His soldiers raided the stronghold, drove off great herds of cattle, and then seized Moshesh's principal wife and other women. Sekonyela seated himself in Moshesh's chair of state. The infuriated Basuto attacked the Batlakoa soldiers so fiercely that they drove them right through the herds of cattle and out at the other side. The Basuto women flung themselves on the ground and embarrassed the movements of their captors. When Moshesh returned he deeply resented Sekonyela's treachery, but instead of seeking revenge he sent a letter to Sekonyela which utterly shamed him, and with it a present of cattle.

Another war incident characteristic of Moshesh is this. The Matebele came again on the scene, not this time to dislodge the enemies of

the Basuto but to attack the Basuto themselves.
They came in force and camped within sight
beneath the mountain, preparing for assault.
While they bathed in the stream and danced and
donned their war ornaments, the tribesmen in
the mountain fortress made ready piles of rock
to launch on their assailants' heads. The Matebele charged up the steep gulleys; masses of rock
hurled downward and a flight of assegais gave
them check. Again and again they were re-
pelled. Finally they struck camp and withdrew.
Then a man from Moshesh stood before them.
"Moshesh salutes you," he said. "Supposing that
hunger brought you to his country, he sends
some cattle to feed you on your journey home."

There is a delightful sequel. Years afterward
a missionary from Basutoland met some Matebele in Cape Town and enquired whether Moshesh was known to them. "Known to us?"
they replied. "Yes. He is the man who, having
rained down rocks on our heads, sent us oxen
for food. We will never attack him again."
And they never did.

Moshesh was a man of wide outlook who saw
far ahead. It was not only fellow-Bantu who
threatened his little state. White men were beginning to press northward in search of land and

new homes.   He knew he could not grapple with
them alone.   But he had heard of other white
men, missionaries, who cared for the interests
of black men.   He would seek for a missionary
of his own.

The romantic story has often been told.
Adam Krotz, a half-caste Griqua Christian from
Philippolis on the Orange River, was brought to
see Moshesh by two Basuto who had met him on
a hunting trip.   Moshesh complained of the
frequent fighting which troubled him; Adam
Krotz replied that he and his people lived in
peace.   "Have you many guns?" queried
Moshesh.   "No, but we have a missionary," replied Krotz.   "That is what you need, Moshesh,
not guns."   Here was a clew indeed.   Moshesh
pleaded with Krotz to get a missionary to come
to him.   Krotz promised to do what he could.

Meantime three young Frenchmen were on
their way to reinforce a mission already begun
by French Protestants.   When they reached the
Cape, Dr. John Philip made known to them
that the station to which they were going had
been attacked and broken up.   He sent the three
disappointed recruits on to Dr. Moffat at Kuruman to await instructions from France.   On
their way they paused at Philippolis just when

Adam Krotz returned from Basutoland, and Krotz told the story of Moshesh. Their call and opportunity had come. Eagerly the missionaries went forward to Thaba Bosiu, to be Moshesh's "men of prayer."

There is a winning artlessness in the journal of young Casalis as he tells of his approach to the mountain stronghold, and of his first interview with the chief. It is evident that the French youth—he was only twenty-one—found a touch of home in the welcome Moshesh gave him, in his playful ways with children, and in the kindliness of Mamahoto his wife.

Two old pictures are extant of Moshesh. One, said to be drawn from life, shows him unclad except for a few decorations; the other is a grotesque photograph of a man in a loose cloak and a high black silk hat. The best likeness of him is the word picture Casalis sent to Paris when first the two men met. "The chief," he said, "bent upon me a look at once majestic and benevolent. His profile was much more aquiline than that of most of his subjects. His well-formed forehead, the fullness and regularity of his features, and his eyes—a little weary but full of intelligence and softness—made a deep impression on me. I felt at once that I had to do with a superior man, trained to think, to command others, and above all to control himself."

Thus opened a great chapter in the adventure of the Christian church. A suitable location was assigned for the mission, well-watered so that new and useful crops might be introduced. More missionaries came, schools were opened, and in the course of years a living Christian community grew up (see p. 181). From the outset Moshesh apprehended the force of the new message. He welcomed it for his people, though he would not personally commit himself until he saw how it worked out. It was, he astutely said, like an egg; he would wait till it was hatched.

But he had found the friends he sought. His missionaries gave him wise and conciliatory advice. They explained ways of Western people which he could not have understood. They wrote his despatches to government officials, though the decisions taken and the phrases used were his own. They delighted in his gallant courage, in his kindly wisdom, in his administrative genius, in his genuine human friendship. The happy relations did honor to all concerned.

As years went by the conditions surrounding Moshesh became more complex. Changes in

Cape Colony led the Boers, as we have already seen, in large numbers to trek northward into the regions devastated by Tshaka's wars. The proper boundary of Basutoland was a matter of debate. Moshesh was willing to welcome settlers as his guests, but when they treated lands as derelict which he claimed as his own, troubles inevitably arose. To make things worse, parties of undisciplined men raided and foraged for themselves; relations between the trekking Boers and the British authorities at the Cape were also strained and uncertain. Sometimes soldiers were sent up on punitive expeditions, and there was actual war. At intervals governors and high officials came to confer about treaties, agreements, boundary maps, and other intricacies of civilization.

Moshesh was generally at issues with the Boers, but for long he stood high in the estimation of the British officials with whom he dealt. He was clear-sighted and conciliatory to an unusual degree. One governor of the Cape described him as "the most enlightened and upright chief in South Africa, worthy of perfect confidence and respect." Moshesh strove to consolidate the Bantu people and draw them into a common bond against the aggression of the new settlers.

He also appealed frequently to the authorities at the Cape and even to England's Queen for help. This was sometimes given, sometimes withheld. Though Moshesh when driven to fight was generally successful, peace and friendship meant far more to him than victory.

The famous story of the battle of Berea shows equally the problems which beset the chief and his wisdom in the hour of success. There was a new governor at the Cape. The Boers had made bitter complaint that the Basuto were raiding on an extensive scale. This was probably true, though it was against the will of the chief. Restitution and a heavy fine were demanded by the authorities; troops were sent across the Berea Mountain to enforce payment from the Basuto. The demand was for ten thousand head of cattle and one thousand horses within three days. The French missionaries support the statement of Moshesh that it was absolutely impossible to comply. The animals could not be brought together in the time. Moshesh sent about a third of what was demanded and then awaited events.

Troops from the Cape, starting from near the little mission station which nestles under Thaba Bosiu, advanced against him in three columns. One got into an ambush and had to retreat, carrying with it great herds of cattle; another was repulsed in an attack; the rest of the troops spent the night among the rocks. In the morning, the prospects of success being uncertain, they were called back to their base camp. The Basuto, fully armed, marched along the ridge of Berea Mountain watching their assailants retreat across the plain. Possibly the tribesmen felt trimphant. But Moshesh was of another mind. His people had been in the wrong over the raiding and no success of arms made it right. In the middle of the night he called a missionary and wrote to the governor thus:

Thaba Bosiu
Midnight, December 20, 1852

YOUR EXCELLENCY:

This day you have fought against my people and taken much cattle. As the object for which you have come is to have a compensation for the Boers, I beg you will be satisfied with what you have taken. I entreat peace from you. You have chastised; let it be enough, I pray you; and let me be no longer considered an enemy to the Queen. I will try all I can to keep my people in order for the future.

Your humble servant,
MOSHESH

The governor ordered the army to march homeward and did not renew the attack. Some have said the governor was wrong to accept the olive branch held out by Moshesh. Few today would agree with that judgment of his act.

In later years, when Basutoland was pressed on every side, Moshesh gained the reputation of crookedness. His instinct of self-preservation was unduly heightened. But, as Sir Godfrey Lagden points out, "the times were crooked." Moshesh certainly did not always keep his engagements or fulfil the undertakings he had given. But, as the same experienced administrator comments, "broken pledges were not his alone." The sturdy independence of Basutoland which Moshesh so ably upheld was unwelcome to many. So was the persistence with which he piloted his little state until it was taken under the direct protection of the British Crown and saved from absorption into local political areas. Not until the closing days of his life did Moshesh learn that this which he so fervently desired had come to pass.

Within Basutoland Moshesh was a wise administrator who ruled his independent and somewhat turbulent people justly and well. He gave them sound laws, he advanced education, he furthered trade, he protected rights in land, he checked the liquor traffic. He trained his people to consider public affairs and to give advice concerning them. Under him the *pitso* or national council became a power—with modified functions it is still at work. He sought nothing for his private ends. Failure in constructive work at home might well have been condoned in view of the constant claims of harrassing external relations. But Moshesh in his practical work as chief ranks high. His record can scarcely be surpassed by any unlettered man, for he was thrown into circumstances of extreme difficulty under which white administrators have proved insufficient again and again.

Moshesh was venerated by his people and reigned unchallenged among them till near the close of his days. Then, weak, aged and half blind, his powers failed him and he was no longer able to grasp affairs. His strenuous life had used up his splendid force at last. For a time he knew a period of eclipse like that of the great Askia. His sons—who never equalled him in character or influence—took the lead in affairs. The old man moved about, a pathetic wreck of kingly greatness. In 1870 he died, being well over seventy years of age. Then his light again shone clear. The Basuto recounted the prowess through which he had made them a nation. They recalled the unselfish service of their chief. The spent old man who had stood in the way of youth became a hero once more. Moshesh reigned again in the hearts of his people. He reigns there still.

VII. KHAMA THE GOOD

A GLANCE at the map shows that while Tshaka's territory centered in Natal and that of Moshesh in Basutoland, the territory of Khama's tribe, the Bamangwato, lay northward outside the Union of South Africa in what is now the protectorate of Bechuanaland. Khama was thus outside the problems created for Moshesh by colonies and republics.

In point of time, Khama was born in or about the year of Tshaka's death, when Moshesh was about thirty years of age. Khama did not become paramount chief until after Moshesh had died. In brief, Moshesh lived from about 1790 to 1870, Khama from about 1828 to 1923.

Khama is generally classed as the finest and most lovable of the many notable African chiefs. He certainly gained little from heredity or from the early surroundings of his life. His father, Sekhome, renowned as a devotee of the diviners and their arts, was satisfactory neither as man nor chief, though he had a large following in the tribe. Sekhome's brother, Macheng,

Khama's uncle, was less estimable still. Family dissension dogged Khama's footsteps throughout all his early days. The jealousy of a father towards his heir—so common in Africa—dominated Sekhome's mind and found expression in unkind actions. Yet even from his father Khama compelled reluctant admiration, whether for his physical prowess or for his character and noble life. "I believe Khama has a white heart," he said one day.

When Khama was about fourteen, Livingstone paid a visit to Shoshong and had talk with the lad. Dr. Robert Moffat came three years afterwards. Later still Khama went to stay with Sechele, chief of the Bakwena, Livingstone's convert and friend, a man of ability and energy who was fighting a brave battle for his hard-pressed tribe. Here Khama saw what Christianity could do for chief and people. He began to learn to read and write. On his return home he won Sekhome to wish for missionaries; if other chiefs had them, why not he? In 1858 a German missionary came to Shoshong, the Bamangwato capital, and Khama, Khamane his brother, and others after due teaching were baptized. Subsequently the work was taken over by the London Missionary Society. Such men as John

Mackenzie,[1] the statesman missionary, and John Smith Moffat and W. C. Willoughby and others in their turn were sent to Shoshong. The Bamangwato did well in missionaries.

Baptized in 1862, Khama became a sincere and intelligent Christian. The Christian conception of marriage strongly appealed to him. He chose a fine Christian girl, whose name, Mogatsumocwasele, was happily superseded for practical purposes by the title Ma-Bessie, and together they built a home full of refinement and love. A white trader visited Khama as his children began to grow up around him and was captivated by his home.

"Khama's home," he wrote, "remains completely African in its surroundings, and is full of refinement and courtesy. I shall always remember the pretty scene we shared in there on our last evening in Shoshong. The large brown hut, its walls stencilled, with broad eaves covering the stoep, made a pleasant shade. The wide clean court was shut in by loopholed walls. By the fire in one corner three little brown maidens were half-playing, half-cooking. At intervals girls with graceful figures crossed the courtyard

---

[1] President Douglas Mackenzie, of Hartford Theological Seminary, has written a fine life of his great father. Since 1919 Professor W. C. Willoughby has also been on the Hartford staff.

carrying corn. Khama's son, a bright gentle-manly boy, sat near his mother, Ma-Bessie, under the eaves, the daughters beside her, the little grandchildren running up to her. Among them was the tall slight man, his thin nervous face full of decision and sweetness, who had won through endurance and peril the purity of that almost unique home among African chiefs."

In truth, Khama from the first budding of his splendid manhood—he was well over six feet, with a frame like whipcord, the swiftest runner, the surest hunter, and the finest rider in the tribe, full of dignity in his bearing yet gentle and winsome as a child—had no easy time. When Sekhome found that Khama would not support the initiation school and discounted all the sorcerers' claims, his anger rose. It swelled to fury when Khama stoutly refused to take a second wife. He was willing, he said, to meet any test of endurance or obedient service his father set, but Ma-Bessie was his one true wife and he would not go against the law of God.

Then began a series of threats and attacks which Khama withstood or foiled. A British general who knew him well wrote of him after his death: "Khama was a grand man—in the tribal and family feuds, when deeply grieved and

injured by the harsh treatment of his father . . .
he showed a Christian strength of character,
humbleness of mind, patience and generosity,
that clearly signalled him as a leader of men. He
reminded us of the conduct of David when pursued by Saul. . . . He showed all the instincts
of a Christian gentleman."

Khama and his younger brother Khamane
shared the weight of their father's displeasure
and often went in danger of their lives. One
night Sekhome posted his armed soldiers round
the huts of his sons and bade them fire. The
men refused to obey. Sekhome, expecting
vengeance, fled; the sons sent him messages of
forgiveness. Believing in the power of his sorcerers, Sekhome then set a group of them to
work. Khama was roused by a flare of light outside his house—the sorcerers were working incantations against him over a fire. Khama
quickly crossed his courtyard in shadow and
suddenly rose to his full height by the splut-
tering fire. The sorcerers incontinently fled.
Having scattered the embers, Khama returned to
sleep. A few months later Sekhome, who had
been sedulously cultivating the Bamangwato
and had got a party on his side, planned another
night attack. Khama heard of it, and he and his

brother simply led the Christians and their cattle on to the hills and stayed there, until, after a little desultory fighting, Sekhome took them back on proper terms.

Macheng, Khama's uncle, who had long been in banishment, now appeared on the scene. In a foolish moment Sekhome had offered him the chieftainship—to which, indeed, he had prior right—if he would kill Khama and Khamane. Macheng was glad to replace his brother as chief, but to Sekhome's dismay he refused to slay his nephews and rather inclined to treat them as friends. Sekhome reverted to his old habit of plotting, but Macheng made short work of him and drove him out. Ere long Macheng found that the ways of Khama were a rebuke to himself and he turned against the two young men. He tried charms and incantations, then he tried to poison them. Things went from bad to worse. At last Khama, seeing the ruin that was coming upon the tribe, appealed for help to Sechele, who was always his friend. Sechele sent warriors who quickly expelled Macheng and would have shot him had not Khama intervened. Macheng, like Sekhome, went into exile and ultimately drank himself to death. Khama was, on his uncle's deposition, elected chief of the Bamangwato in September 1872.

One more interlude lay between Khama and settled rule. Against the judgment of Sechele, he invited his father to return as chief. Perhaps he hoped that the needed lesson had been learned. If so, he was soon undeceived. Sekhome accepted the invitation, began the same old plotting, and heaped insult after insult on Khama's head until it was impossible to go on. Then Khama made a characteristic move. He quietly departed from Shoshong and trekked forty miles northward to Serowe. Those who chose him as chief could follow him, he said. In a few days men, women, children and cattle were on trek for Serowe, and there were five thousand empty huts in Shoshong. Sekhome carried on miserably for a time in Shoshong, then Khama appeared before the town and his father fled. Khama was henceforth paramount chief.

Travelers and missionaries vie with each other in testimony to the influence of Khama's doings. Administrators bear witness that the highest qualities of leadership were his. Religion was central in the life of his people, and Khama was scrupulously fair to those whose opinions differed from his own. He had foresworn polygamy, he abhorred sorcery and the diviners' arts, he disbelieved in the rain-makers, he held the influence and methods of the initiation school to be hurtful. Neither as man nor as chief would he countenance these things. All religious functions in the *kotla* became Christian. Khama himself conducted two services there every Sunday, standing beneath the ancient tree of justice with the open sky overhead. The heathen rites at time of harvest were displaced by Christian prayer and thanksgiving. Yet no compulsion was used. Unlike Sechele, who in his early days with Livingstone wanted to make the Bakwena Christians by use of his hippopotamus whip, Khama knew that any changes worth having must begin in the heart.

The chief set himself to establish order throughout his land. Thieving ceased so completely that travelers set no night watch on their wagons when they camped on Khama's ground. A traveler [2] at first prejudiced against Khama wrote after a week spent in his capital:

"Khama has established peace, prosperity, and justice in all his borders. His word is law. He pervades everything in his town. He is always

[2] *The Ruined Cities of Mashonaland,* by J. T. Bent, London, 1892, pp. 23-27.

on horseback visiting the fields, the stores and
the outlying kraals. He has a word for everyone: he calls every woman 'my daughter' and
every man 'my son,' he pats the little children
on the head. He is a veritable father of his
people, a curious and unaccountable outcrop of
mental power and integrity amongst a degraded
and powerless race. . . . Perhaps he may be said
to be the only Negro living whose biography
would repay the writing." From the last sentence it is hoped that readers of *Sons of Africa*
will dissent.

In commenting on the reality of Khama's
Christianity, one of the leading newspapers of
South Africa cited his attitude to the Marsawa
(Bushmen) and the Bakalakari as illustration.
No other African ruler cared for these despised
and downtrodden desert-dwellers as did he.
Many of them lived within the boundaries of his
tribe. Even the Christians at first called them
not people but dogs without souls. Khama, in
referring to a Bushman, said "one of my people."
He punished those who treated them cruelly; he
even tried to evoke their manhood by showing
confidence in them. He gave some of them a
few goats to tend for him, but found, as he told
a missionary, that it was not a great success for

the Bushmen and was still less of a success for the goats. Yet his kindly treatment did call out response. A Bushman who formerly spoke of himself as "your dog" was heard to say one day, "I, I am a person."

Khama and his missionaries were on excellent terms, working together for the welfare of the tribe. The intimacy was sometimes more like that which exists between men with a common racial heritage. In particular, by virtue of the love and purity of his own home life and his ideals of Christian womanhood, Khama entered into the sanctities of the white man's family life.

"It is now nearly a quarter of a century since Khama and I became friends," writes a missionary's wife. "For months at a time, when my husband was visiting the Lake Ngami people, have I been left with my children under Khama's sole protection and guardianship. No brother could have cared for us more thoughtfully and kindly. In all our intercourse I can most gratefully say that he was to me always a true Christian gentleman in word and deed. No one now living knows 'Khama the Good' as I know him. Did they do so, they would both honor and trust him as I do."

Things, of course, were not always smooth.

Khama could be very autocratic and determined; once his confidence was lost it was not easy to regain. Once or twice he parted in displeasure from a loyal friend who had served him well. But few men in a position of sole leadership walk perfectly, whether their lot be cast in Africa or elsewhere.

Two great moral battles on behalf of his tribe were fought by Khama, one to abolish drink in his territories, the other to secure the land for the people.

One of Khama's missionaries, now Professor W. C. Willoughby, learned from the chief's own lips what first turned him into a determined prohibitionist. His decision was taken after a sorry scene with his father. Sekhome wanted to buy a horse from a trader who had outspanned near by. He invited the young Khama to go with him, and five fine tusks of ivory were taken to pay for the horse. The trader was a worthless and designing man. Khama saw with dismay that he was giving more and more brandy to Sekhome. At last the trader tried to induce the chief to part with all the ivory for a little powder and two bars of lead. Sekhome never allowed his sons to interfere with him, and his temper was dangerous when it was roused. But Khama could not stand by and see his father cheated and dishonored, and as Sekhome was fast becoming quite incapable, Khama ordered the servants to pick up the intoxicated chief and carry him and the ivory home. Khama knew there would be trouble for him next morning. But he told the missionary afterwards that as he walked home behind the servants and their miserable burden he took a resolution that he would henceforth fight against drink as long as he lived.

When he came into power a number of unworthy traders were resident in the tribe, drinking heavily and supplying strong liquor to the Bamangwato. Khama believed in trade and welcomed right-minded white traders. Some of them have recorded how much they owed to his friendship and his generous help in time of need. But the kind of traders Sekhome had encouraged, men enriching themselves by undermining the morals of the tribe, were detestable in Khama's eyes. A law against the importation and sale of spirits was enacted and made public after he came to the throne. Those who profited by the sale of drink protested, but in vain; Khama stuck to his resolve. Then they tried smuggling; Khama, who knew most things that happened, exposed their misdeeds.

At last the traders resolved to force matters by
defying the chief. They met and had a wild
carouse, but things went further than they expected, for drinking led to fighting, there was a
noisy brawl, and Khama himself was summoned
to the spot and, with one of his missionaries, saw
the disgraceful orgy. Two days later the culprits were summoned before him. His stern
words cut like whips. The traders pleaded for
mercy; Khama replied that his mercy was needed
for the tribe whom God had committed to his
care. The traders were allowed to gather their
possessions and were expelled from the chief's
borders forever. "I am black, but I am chief in
my own country," he said. "I rule, and shall
maintain my laws."

After sixteen years of chieftainship, Khama
wrote to a high official, "To fight against drink
is to fight against demons and not against men.
I dread the white man's drink more than all the
assegais of the Matebele." Not only did he stop
the importation of spirits but he forbade the
making of Kaffir beer. In this some of his white
friends—missionaries and officials—thought he
went too far. At one time his life was in danger
from the indignation of some of the younger

men of the tribe. But his conviction held against all opposition and he carried the day.

The fight made by Khama to save the land for his tribe is one of the most stirring episodes in South African history. Other chiefs south of the Zambesi, tempted by one lure or another, granted freehold rights to white men. Khama never parted with an acre of his tribal lands to settlers. When he welcomed the formal establishment of the British Protectorate in 1885 he made conditions reserving not only the ownership of land but the right to decide all cases arising among his people by customary law, and to maintain existing legislation against intoxicating liquor. He agreed to fight beside the British if need arose, and kept his promise in the Matebele war of 1892.

The breaking of the Matebele power cleared a way for the great schemes of the Chartered Company. Cecil Rhodes definitely aspired to absorb Khama's country and other neighboring regions into its sphere. This Khama resisted with all his might. He and two other African chiefs visited England under missionary escort in 1895 and put their case before the government. "Against them," writes one of

Khama's biographers,[3] "were the map-makers with their red-paint brush, the speculators with their share-scrip, the party politicians with their place-hunting opportunism, and the man in the street with colossal and complacent ignorance of the whole subject." But in the end the three chiefs won. The Secretary of State for the Colonies gave his final decision in their favor. During Khama's visit to England the gentleness and dignity of his manhood enabled those who met him to envisage what an African can be.

In 1889 the supply of water at Shoshong proved insufficient, and Khama in true African fashion led all his people, with their goods and cattle, to Palapye, one hundred miles to the northeast. It was a three-days' journey and the trek took months to complete. The new town, as Khama planned it, covered twenty square miles and each of its ten divisions had a well-ventilated schoolroom. Unhappily Palapye did not prove a good site, so in 1902 the tribe moved again to Serowe, a distance of about forty-five miles. Serowe still serves as the center of their tribal life.

As many will remember, Khama had a glorious jubilee of his chieftainship in the summer of

[3] J. C. Harris, in *Khama, the Great African Chief*, p. 89.

1922. Congratulations were heaped upon him as missionaries, government officials, and tribesmen in a great assembly bore testimony to the qualities of the chief. Khama himself, hale and full of vigor, made a great speech, the longest ever heard from his lips in Serowe. He recounted the blessings which the gospel had brought; he expressed his gratitude to the white men who were his friends and had come to do him honor; he closed with straight and fearless Christian counsel to his tribe:

"Let these words enter your hearts. . . . Depart from disputes, think like men, seek to know the road, let your hearts depart from drink and from the initiation ceremonies; get to know the true knowledge about marriage, that it is an oath before God."

Khama's long life was to end less than a year later, in February 1923. He was over ninety years of age. He still enjoyed his daily ride on horseback and held his wonted place in the councils of the tribe. Ma-Bessie had died, beloved and honored; Semane, who had filled her place and survived Khama, carried on the new tradition of married life. Except that his eldest son did not walk in the ways of his father, Khama's home was full of light and peace. Problems still gathered round his people and ceaseless vigilance was required to guard them, both from their enemies and from themselves. There was always a party in opposition to the chief. Yet his was a singularly fair old age, rich and fruitful to the last. Caught in a rain storm when out riding, and severely chilled, the old man felt his strength rapidly fail. After a few days, surrounded by love and honor, he gradually grew weaker and peacefully died.

He was buried on a hilltop above Serowe. The monument erected there to his memory, unveiled with full honors by the Prince of Wales in 1925, bears as inscription on its base: "Righteousness exalteth a nation."

VIII. SIR APOLO KAGWA: FROM PAGE TO PRIME MINISTER

SIR APOLO KAGWA died in February 1927, at the comparatively early age of sixty-two. Yet the great prime minister of Uganda had seen marvelous changes in his day. Except for one visit to England, his life lay entirely in Uganda in the service of three successive kings. In the days of Kabaka Mutesa, the king in whose time the white men first came and Christianity found entrance, Kagwa was a page at court. In the days of Kabaka Mwanga, Mutesa's weaker son—who ended his life in banishment in the Seychelles Islands, having persecuted the Christians, ordered the murder of Bishop Hannington, and pursued a policy so vacillating that he alienated every party in turn—Kagwa was, first, page; then bearer of the king, an office for which by strength and stature he was fitted; then royal storekeeper; and, finally, general of the king's army and Katikiro, or prime minister. Under Kabaka Daudi Chwa, who in his infancy succeeded his father, Mwanga, on the throne and is happily still living, Kagwa was one of the three regents appointed to rule during the minority of the king. He continued to hold this office, also the office of Katikiro, even after Daudi Chwa attained his majority in 1914, and only laid it down shortly before his death. His term of office covered thirty-five years.

Uganda in the period covered by Kagwa's lifetime offered a worthy sphere for a man of strength. Mutesa had behind him more than thirty generations of royal blood. The country, attractive in many of its natural features, was off the track of traders from other lands. The civilization which characterized it was entirely its own. Sir Frederick (now Lord) Lugard, whose knowledge of Africa is varied, says, "So far as we are aware, no purely pagan tribe in Africa, shut off from contact with surrounding peoples on a higher plane of civilization, has ever developed so extraordinary a social, political and even legal system as was found at the time of its discovery in Uganda."

When Speke, searching for the source of the Nile, reached Uganda in 1862 he found a complex system of social organization, much of which has been continued in the life and local government of Uganda today. The people were intelligent and well-mannered, clad in beautiful soft brown bark cloth, their bodies unmarred by the mutilations common in other tribes. Their manufactures were admirable, they gave attention to farming, they owned herds and flocks. They were brave and they were given to fighting; indeed, neighboring tribes found their warlike qualities much in excess.

The vivid detailed journals of Speke's stay at the Uganda court reflect conditions of self-indulgence and capriciousness, but Mutesa was then a young man, he lacked the discipline of life, and the influence of the queen-mother's court was not bracing. Cruel practices were common; the moral tone was low. When Stanley, who as a young man had been previously sent by the New York *Herald* to find Livingstone, came to Uganda twelve years later, he found Mutesa greatly improved though still cruel and lacking in self-restraint. A Moslem teacher had helped him; Stanley began to teach him the Christian faith, and in 1875 stirred the Christian world by the letter in which he appealed for a Christian mission to Uganda. In Mutesa he saw a future Christian monarch influencing the heart of Africa.

Promptly, in 1877, the Church Missionary

Society sent out a party; the French Roman Catholics followed in 1879. Among the early missionaries were some notable men. They won, as Stanley had foreseen, an immediate response, though Mutesa did not become its leader. The Baganda flocked to listen and to learn, especially the bright lads whose faculties had been quickened by responsible duties at court. Here the first mention of the future prime minister is found. One of the king's pages, "young Kagwa," grandson of a county chief in Bulewezi, came with others to be taught.

Mutesa died, a king who had stood at the crossways where old Uganda ended and new Uganda was to come into being. Mwanga, his son, came to power. At first he was interested in the two religions, Islam and Christianity, which were impinging on the old paganism of Uganda. Then he suddenly turned against them both. For the Christians a fierce persecution began, led by the king himself. Young Kagwa, now a baptized member of the little church, raised his voice in protest. He was almost slain by Mwanga and bore the mark of his master's hand all his days.

The flame of persecution burned fiercely till the whole world knew of the Uganda martyrdoms, but the people still pressed in to be taught. To this day Christians come to the holy communion whose lips were cut off in Mwanga's days as a punishment for their confession of faith. Apolo Kagwa—he now had a Christian name— was quite bold about his faith; nothing but his usefulness saved him from death. Mwanga came to depend on him more and more, both in war and in affairs of state.

As the last decade of the nineteenth century drew near, internal dissension became acute and international influences swept into Central Africa. Three parties within Uganda were struggling for ascendancy; they bore religious names but were really political at bottom. The Mohammedan party was strong and assertive, backed by Kabarega, king of Bunyoro, himself a Moslem; the Christians, now grown numerous and influential, were in two groups: the English (Bangreza) or Protestant, the French (Bafranza) or Roman Catholic. It was a shock to find what looked like religious war breaking out in Central Africa.

Meantime European powers were penetrating Africa. Situations strained and perilous arose between them more than once. Representatives of Germany and of England approached

Mwanga. He accepted the advances of both.   At last, in the year 1890, it was agreed in a treaty between the two rival powers that Uganda lay within the African sphere of Great Britain.   The Imperial British East Africa Company carried on work till 1894, when Uganda became a British protectorate.

All through these years Mwanga hesitated and intrigued with one party after another; the friend of one year was the foe of the next. Against the background of confusion and recurring wars two figures stand out boldly: Captain (afterwards Lord) Lugard, acting for the British with the patience and wisdom which marked him out as a great colonial administrator; and the African prime minister and general, working with the British official yet striving to be loyal to his degenerate king.   Neither in religious nor political affairs did Apolo Kagwa hide his convictions.   He was frankly of opinion that the future of his country lay in accepting partnership with the British rather than with any other power, and he saw there was no hope that Uganda, torn by internal divisions, could stand alone.   He steered his way through the conflicting currents by keeping his country's welfare in view.   When the Imperial British

East Africa Company was succeeded by a full British protectorate, he encouraged Mwanga and the people to welcome the change. But he never surrendered the right of private judgment. He was a far-seeing and reasonable man, who bent every energy to understand and grapple with a situation. What he said was always heard with respect and often proved to be sound.

At last it became impossible to prop up Mwanga any longer. He had forfeited the confidence of his own people as well as of the British officials now on the scenes. He was ruining Uganda, and in the eyes of Kagwa that was the final crime. Mwanga was deported to the Seychelles Islands in 1901, and Uganda has ever since been at peace.

The country quickly settled down under the new régime. Three regents, of whom Kagwa was one, were appointed to act for the infant king. As regent and Katikiro as well, Kagwa had the leading place. Sir H. H. Johnston was sent out as commissioner; in conference with him the Uganda Agreement was drawn up in 1900. In it questions of land, law, and taxations were dealt with; much of the time-honored system of government was carried forward into the new day; the *lukiko* or national assembly with its representative membership was continued, and to it important functions were assigned; the position of the chiefs, graded as in former years, was confirmed and where necessary readjusted in conference with the Baganda themselves. Subject to final reference to the British authorities, the local and county courts under selected chiefs and their assessors were left to deal with all Native cases except those involving the death penalty. In all this settlement and the administrative work which followed, Kagwa took the foremost place. Sometimes, on state occasions, the little boy king sat in the chair of state in the *lukiko,* but always with the Katikiro by his side.

At the time of the coronation of Edward VII in 1902 the Katikiro was invited to take part in the celebrations in London as the official representative of Uganda. He filled his place with dignity; he was present at the great service in Westminster Abbey; he was received at Buckingham Palace by the newly crowned King. During a stay of several months' duration he visited centers of industry and gained experience for his country. He was popular and received hospitality from many famous men. His dignity, his fine person, and his intelligence were a credit to his race. Ham Mukasa, a chief of standing and of high repute among Christians in Uganda, came with him as secretary. The two Africans night by night talked over the wonders of the day. Ham Mukasa wrote a fine volume recording their experiences, which was read both in Uganda and in England.

Before turning to some of the less public aspects of Sir Apolo Kagwa's life, the testimony which shows him as one of the forces that have shaped the new Uganda must find place. He enjoyed the confidence of one British official after another; he stood with them in constructive effort for his country's good. "His race," to quote from one of the leading English papers, "may claim that, entering the world of written history but yesterday, it has already produced a statesman." An official who had seen him at work in Uganda wrote in the London *Morning Post* at the time of his death:

"To be prime minister of so progressive a country as Uganda is no light task. To rule over an enlightened Native parliament calls for qualities and brains of no mean order. He framed rules and procedures which enable his countrymen to take a hand at governing themselves—to dispense laws and justice to their own people, in their own cabinet, with their own parliament."

There is always a stir of interest when a book is written in which the personal life and character of a well-known statesman are discussed. No life has yet been written of Sir Apolo Kagwa, but friends both British and African love to talk of him.

Large of stature, broad in build, erect in carriage, he was an impressive figure, especially in his robes of state. His expression was stern, at times almost forbidding, until his roving eyes caught sight of a friend. Then his face lit with sudden recognition and broke into a pleasant smile. His friendliness was eager and forthgoing and expressed itself in innumerable forms. Hospitality was a delight to him, and his beautiful house was used to the full. Whether it was a smart reception with a gold-edged invitation card for some distinguished stranger, or an African wedding party having a feast on his lawn, or a crowd of high school boys come for a good afternoon, the Katikiro was happy if he had guests. Samali, his wife, though a friend of the women missionaries, preferred to remain in charge of the household out of sight. A worthy woman of the older school, she never took the social place so natural to the young Kabaka's charming wife, the Lady Irene.

Sir Apolo was a generous giver, whether to causes or to individuals in need. The schools and the medical work of the mission called out his gifts; to one of the buildings of the great cathedral at Namirembe he gave thirty per cent of his own rentals from land for several years, and collected similar sums from the chiefs. He liked to give those nice, not absolutely necessary things that cause special pleasure. The Mukono Training College, for instance, owed to him the fine four-faced striking clock in its tower.

Himself a student of the history and folklore of his country—on which he wrote two excellent books in the vernacular, one of them just republished in the year of his death—he liked to foster the work of others and to cooperate with students from the West. One of the missionaries named Roscoe, a well-known anthropologist, acknowledges in the preface of a scientific volume how much he owed to the Katikiro's help. His large house was thrown open; elder people who knew the religious practices and folklore of their country were sought out; if old and feeble, they were carried it might be a hundred miles, that in the comfort and quiet of

Sir Apolo's home they might yield to the scholar the treasures of the past. And the busy statesman found time to draw upon his boyhood's memories, sketching a great plan, which duly appears in one of the volumes, of Mutesa's palace and its surroundings, where he had been a little white-robed page.

He who had never gone to school not only gave his own sons a first-rate modern education but furthered schools in Uganda for boys and girls. He believed in higher education for women. He served on the education board of the diocese; he knew nearly every boy in the Mengo Boys' High School; he read their essays; he followed their examination work; above all he loved the prize day with its awards. The great mission hospital, with its training of nurses and assistants and its far-flung preventive work, lay equally within his ken.

He was in touch with questions of social reform. He, with forty other chiefs, drew up and signed a document giving liberty to all their slaves. He cared about better houses and sanitation for the people. He knew the value of publicity, and got out a little printing-press from England from which he issued pamphlets on subjects useful to farmers in rural areas. He believed in manual labor and in industrial work. He sometimes gave a lesson in bricklaying or carpentry, and when clay was needed for one of the earlier cathedrals—before the present beautiful brick building was erected—he joined the long stream of men, women, and children carrying clay to the site, the only difference being that his load was heavier than the rest.

On Thursday afternoons, year after year, Sir Apolo had in his house a Bible class for chiefs, led by one of the missionaries. It began as soon as the session of the *lukiko* closed. Chiefs on foot or on bicycles, or even, latterly, in automobiles were to be seen streaming up his avenue, sometimes to the number of sixty or seventy. The missionaries who used to attend it will remember that Bible class all their lives.

A little over sixty when he died, what amazing changes those penetrating eyes of Sir Apolo Kagwa had seen in the country he loved and served! And how large a part he himself had played in bringing them about!

In his lifetime Uganda had stepped from almost complete isolation into the wider world, still keeping a distinctive character of its own. Means of communication had multiplied; a railway running from coast to lake, and steamboats crossing the wide waters, replaced the human porterage, the weary march of months, the canoes on the perilous lake. Trade was no longer a matter of slaves and ivory, but increasing export and import on a worldwide scale. The medicine men with their charms and ordeals were being routed; the customs which darkened the lot of women in childbirth were being laid aside; doctors and nurses preaching the gospel of health were training men to fight against disease and conserving infant life. The lore of the village elders and the discipline of tribal life were no longer the sole sources of instruction for youth. When Kagwa was born there was not a school in the whole of Uganda; when he died there was a network of education over all the country—though many of the meshes were far too large—from the myriad little bush schools through the village and central schools for boys and girls, up to the new government college at Makerere in the capital.

Greatest change of all: when Kagwa was born there was no known Christian of Baganda race, nor in all the country any group who worshiped Jesus Christ as Lord. In the year of his death, the Native Anglican Church of Uganda held its jubilee. The diocese, reaching over the borders of Uganda proper and including some of the countries with which Mutesa and his fathers fiercely fought, contains at least 165,000 baptized Christians, an equal number belonging to the Church of Rome. The cathedral which Sir Apolo helped to build and in which he regularly worshiped has two African canons; the story of one of them is told on page 173. In the ministry of the church there are ordained Africans, with a goodly company of teachers, evangelists and schoolteachers, men and women, who have been trained in the schools and colleges he loved.

Sir Apolo Kagwa was not a man of saintly character, like chief Khama or Dr. Kwegyir Aggrey. The faults which marred his public and private life were known to others and to himself. But he was an enlightened and fearless patriot, a man loyal and honorable in his dealings, free from self-seeking and greed, a sincere Christian who made sacrifices for his faith, and one of the ablest of all Africans.

IX. WHERE THREE CONTINENTS MEET: THE LIFE WORK OF J. E. KWEGYIR AGGREY

❦ *Part One.* 1875-1924

WE threaded our way (in Chapter III) among the trading posts on the Gulf of Guinea, watched the wars and shifting alliances of the Fantis and other coastal tribes, and held our breath as the fierce Ashantis swept down upon them from the north. The reek of human sacrifices rose in our nostrils, the complaint of the slave was in our ears; yet we were won to admiration of Osai Tutu Kwamina, the great Ashanti king who died in Kumasi on the day that his armies first defeated a British force. This was in 1824.

We return, a little more than a century later, to a new day on the Gold Coast. Wars have ceased; slavery and the slave trade have faded into the past. Trade, largely in the hands of Native cultivators, prospers. Ashanti is a well-administered and progressive territory, with the beginnings of an adequate educational policy. Prempeh, the last of its long line of kings, is back, after a tragic interlude of banishment, as chief among his people. The years of recurring wars have been succeeded by settled peace, and the blunders which marred the work of Great Britain as a colonizing power have been recognized and forsworn. The story passes through pain to thankfulness; we cannot trace it here.[1] But we pick up one thread which begins early in the nineteenth century and follow it to the present day.

During Tutu Kwamina's reign there grew up on the West Coast a boy named Kodwo Kwegyir Aggrey, descended from a Fanti family whose lineage stretched centuries into the past. The boy became a man of wisdom and influence, disciplined by troublous days. He held the important office of linguist, or royal spokesman. He spoke to and for his master in all national or tribal affairs; it was his to interpret situations, to further or to hinder war. In one terrible quarrel between the people of Cape Coast and Anamabu, Kodwo Aggrey and a group of councillors were called in when the British governor had failed to settle the dispute. The dogs of war strained at their leash. For two days lengthy

[1] For a brief outline, see *The Golden Stool*. For full details, see Claridge's two-volume *History of the Gold Coast*.

statements were made from both sides. Then Kodwo Aggrey rose to review the evidence and present the verdict of his group. He spoke for two hours and never missed a point. Both sides were satisfied and a peaceful agreement was reached.

When the roads between Fanti and Ashanti were closed by war, Kodwo Aggrey could always pass through. He was known and trusted in the courts of both people and never betrayed his trust. He was a warrior, like all the men of his time. But if he was foremost in line of battle he was first to counsel both sides to make peace. As life grew more settled he was the intimate friend of the African men who became leaders in the Gold Coast and took part in administrative work (see p. 156).

To this man in the year 1875 was given a little son, who inherited his father's gifts and character and in after years loved to recall what that father's influence had been. The mother— hale and active at the age of eighty-five as these lines are written—was heir to the stools of five of the local chieftainships. To them her eldest child, this boy, was born inheritor. In early childhood his head was bathed in the sacred spring Kakawa, credited with magic qualities.

Presently he went to school at Cape Coast Castle, the first of his line to be touched by Western education. The friendly Wesleyan missionary discovered his capacity; at fourteen he was employed as a teacher. Later on he had sole charge of a school where one hundred per cent of the pupils passed the government examination. Later still he was a student at Richmond College, a Wesleyan institution on the Gold Coast. He became a Christian and was baptized as James Emman Kwegyir Aggrey. Through his influence, brothers, sisters, mother and father became Christian too. The father came to his boys and said, "You have been Christians longer than I have. Now that I have joined you, tell me what change I should make in my life." So honorable was that life, so pure and peaceful the home, that the boys knew not what to suggest. We do not hear of many pagans like Mohlomi and Kodwo Kwegyir Aggrey; let us thank the Father of Lights for every one.

To the Cape Coast school some workshops were added, and a printing press. This fascinated young Aggrey, as John Tengo Jabavu had been fascinated a few years before (see p. 159), and he learned the trade. In 1896, being able to speak the three principal dialects of the country, he was taken with the British expedition to Kumasi as interpreter, and witnessed the moving scenes at the arrest and deportation of King Prempeh. Not long afterward Aggrey's father peacefully died, at ninety-five years of age. Up to the last the government officials were wont to consult the wise old man on questions of procedure and Fanti customary law. He seems to have had some vision on his deathbed as to his son's future, a vision which remained in that son's memory to the close of his life.

After his father's death young Aggrey went to Accra; thence, under the guidance of Bishop Small of the American Methodist Episcopal Zion Church, he passed to America and entered on the next part of his career. He went south to Salisbury, a town in North Carolina, and in 1898 joined the freshman class at Livingstone College, the leading institution of Bishop Small's church. He proved a brilliant student, taking his A.B. in 1902, when he graduated at the head of a specially able class. To eke out his small resources he worked in vacations as a journalist and in a newspaper office. He became a member of the staff of the college, where he taught for twenty years. He took his M.A. in 1912, and presently his D.D. at Hood Theological Seminary in Salisbury.

In 1905, when he was thirty years of age, he married Rose Rudolph Douglass, an honored graduate of Shaw University, Raleigh, North Carolina, like her husband of African race, and one of a highly respected family long settled in Virginia. Thus was set up another Aggrey home, marked by fellowship and high ideals.

Those were busy years at Salisbury. The teacher's influence was deep and strong; his vivid human sympathy brought him close to his students; many of them were helped by him to pay the fees for their course. He was an ardent preacher, both in rural districts and in towns; his gospel brought religion into touch with daily life. State and central government plans for farm and home demonstration claimed his aid; he was an apostle of health in the neighborhood. Already his qualities as bridge-builder were manifest. The respect of the white people of Salisbury was accorded him; he was a welcome member of the community.

A charming picture of his home in Salisbury is given by a Scottish missionary and his wife who were his guests. "The night we spent in Dr. Aggrey's home in Salisbury we look back on

as one of our best times in America. He had a
beautiful home, dainty and well kept, with its
four public rooms and several bedrooms. His
study was lined with books all round, and one
could see they were a joy to him. A party of
their friends were asked to meet us in the evening and we had a gay time with music and talk
and delightful refreshments. Mrs. Aggrey, such
a capable and charming wife, did nearly everything in the house herself, besides teaching in the
college."

Aggrey's penetrating mind was athirst for
further knowledge. He found his opportunity
in the summer sessions at Columbia University
in New York. To meet the expenses of these
sessions he worked extremely hard and made
heroic sacrifices. He was a student there in
1904, and again in 1914 for the five following
years. His subjects were mainly education and
sociology.

Through all his eager work and study and his
wide participation in American life—it is interesting also to find him in one summer session
studying Japanese—the love of his heart was
with Africa. In 1919 a great door of opportunity opened before him, through the confident
faith in his capacities of his friend, Dr. Thomas

Jesse Jones. An international Commission on
Education in Africa was being sent out by the
Phelps-Stokes Fund, with the support of mission
boards in America and in Europe and the sympathetic interest of many government officials in
Africa and in the British Colonial Office. Dr.
Jones, Educational Director of the Fund, was
Chairman of the Commission. He proposed
that Dr. Aggrey should be made a full member.
Wise heads were shaken at first. Would it not
be embarrassing, owing to customary restric-
tions, to have an African in the party on some
of the boats? In Africa itself might not his
presence make the frank discussion of racial situations difficult when important negotiations
had to be carried through? But hesitancy van-
ished as Dr. Aggrey's attitude and spirit became
known. From beginning to end—in the preliminary arrangements, in the conversations in
Great Britain, in the close personal interrelations
of the members of the Commission and their
confidential discussions, in approach to the Native peoples and in intercourse with government
officials and settlers—the African member was
an unqualified success.

What was he like, the man whom we have
followed from his father's home to the place

where he stands facing distinguished international service? Of good height and slender build, he looks less than his five and forty years. Light in step, graceful in movement, with deft expressive gestures and quick perception of little social courtesies, he adapts himself to any surroundings with simplicity and ease. His mind, like his body, is both disciplined and free, his judgment is sound, his conclusions rapid. He harbors no condemnatory spirit towards any man. He is quiet and gentle in bearing, even at times silent and remote, but his wit can flash and sparkle and his laughter is infectious and gay. In a discussion he waits till the right moment, then he intervenes and in an instant his weight is felt. He bears the mark both of intellectual ability and of gentleness, his smile disarms anger and draws children to his side. In speaking he can play on his audience as on an instrument, yet he is never emotional or cheap.[2] There is a gentle dignity about him which no slight can ruffle, nor does it cloud his simplicity to stand before rulers of men. Allowing full credit for what more

[2] One of the Company officials on the Gold Coast, who was cruelly put to death in 1812, Mr. Meredith of Winneba, has this illuminating description of a Fanti's speech: "To see a Fanti to advantage he must be seen pleading his cause; his words are accompanied with actions by no means ungraceful nor unsuitable to the subject, and his attitudes and energy of expression are highly interesting."

than twenty years of American education has given, he is not the son of that New World in which he built his second home. He is the flower of African Christian manhood as surely as Khama was. To those who knew him best the African note in his mentality not only persisted but increased.

The Commission of 1920-21 visited all the countries of West Africa, in many of which American missions are at work, from Sierra Leone southward; it visited also the Union of South Africa and the Belgian Congo, again touching American work. The aim was to survey the educational needs of the African peoples, including their religious, social and economic welfare and their health, and to discover what further action on the part of missions and governments seemed required. The report published by the Commission on its return made a profound impression. Three years later, in 1924, a second Commission under the same auspices and leadership and with broader support, again included Dr. Aggrey. It visited Abyssinia, all the countries of East and Central Africa and parts of South Africa again. This Commission produced another remarkable report.

Dr. Aggrey's share in the work of the Commission is shown from many different angles. "His humor, sanity, eloquence, knowledge of Native psychology, thorough training in education and sociology, and high Christian purpose, all proved assets of great importance in dealing wisely and constructively with complicated problems and in racial differences"—that is the testimony in the Introduction to the first printed Report. "Though these Commissions included distinguished and capable representatives of the United States and Great Britain," writes the Chairman, "Dr. Aggrey's Native origin, his charming personality, and his powers of inter-racial interpretation enabled him to render services greater than those of any other member. The Native people hung upon his words and accepted his injunctions with almost pathetic eagerness; missionaries believed in him; traders and settlers were impressed by his spirit and wisdom; governments felt that his influence made for the real development of the country and the people."

The great event for Dr. Aggrey, of course, was his return to the Gold Coast and to his mother, like Bishop Crowther's return to the Yoruba country some seventy years before (see

p. 50).   One of the members of the Commission tells of his welcome from his own people after an absence of twenty-two years.

The most vivid picture of him is one at Cape Coast, where he was educated and where his mother still lives.   We came round by coasting steamer from Sekondi and it was dark when we arrived on Cape Coast beach.   There were crowds and crowds to meet Dr. Aggrey.   There was an official dinner for the Education Commission given at the Provincial Commissioner's bungalow that night.   We made haste to get ready, but when the hour came Dr. Aggrey was not there.   After waiting some time, dinner was served.   In the middle Dr. Aggrey appeared, looking rather shy and like a naughty schoolboy.   "I'm very sorry, I couldn't help it," he said.   "You see I *had* to go and see my mother before anyone else."

When we were going on from Cape Coast to Accra we arranged to stop for half an hour at Anamabu, Dr. Aggrey's native place, to greet the chief.   When we got to the entrance of the town we were mysteriously stopped.   Dr. Aggrey had preceded us but was nowhere to be seen.   Suddenly a group appeared from a house near by escorting Dr. Aggrey, who was gorgeously arrayed in full Native costume, and very magnificent he looked.   Out came the Wesleyan schools in full array, lining the roads and gay with flags.   We would have marched right through, but each division as we reached them shouted, "God save the King," and of course we had to stand right through the verse. We had four goes of it. Next appeared a brass band, with more "God save the King"; at last with flags flying we were marched to the tune of Tipperary to the parade ground beside the fort. Here a grand stand was erected, covered with bunting and palm leaves, and opposite to it a great array of chiefs and their followers with many huge state umbrellas. It was a great sight. There were addresses of welcome and speeches; Dr. Aggrey was formally installed into the office of linguist which his father held. Then more speeches and photographs. We felt it a great honor to have been present at this welcome back.

From area after area testimony came to this man's influence. Now and then disagreeable incidents arose; Dr. Aggrey bore them with a smile. In South Africa he won the confidence of the Dutch leaders, especially those of the Dutch Reformed church. "His visit was particularly valuable in the way he was able to commend cooperation between the white and black races," wrote the principal of Lovedale Institution. "His return is looked forward to with satisfaction." [3] "Some of his greatest personal triumphs," wrote another, "were won in the

[3] An invitation was given to join the staff at Fort Hare, quite close to Lovedale. The matter was under consideration when the call to Achimota came.

Transvaal and Johannesburg, where large audiences of astute men, English and Dutch, heard him gladly." His quick perception, his mastery of crowd psychology, his unfailing humor made him a match in public debate for even hostile audiences. He had studied Afrikaans with some Boer students whom he met at Columbia, that he might the better understand South Africans. Some men who had strong views as to the inequality of the black man refused to come to hear him lest they should be compelled to change their minds. An African traveler wrote: "During my last trip through South Africa I heard many and various opinions of Dr. Aggrey, but those of value registered his charm and versatility and paid tribute to his manhood. . . . He was Africa's greatest gift to the world."

From East Africa the record is the same. He won friends among the whole range of people who there seek to work out a common life. In Kenya the wild tribesmen loved him. They called him "our gentleman," and still inquire when he will return. While he was with the Commission he met Lord Delamere and some of the settlers in conference, and afterwards Lord Delamere talked with him on the future of the Native people. In Nyasaland the tribesmen hung upon his words in perfect confidence that he could help them. "When night had fallen and the time had come for him to embark on his boat they clung to his coat and then to his boat, risking the dangers of the alligator-infested waters, that they might have final touch with his personality. Those of us who looked on were sharing an experience never to be forgotten. Thus Aggrey went throughout Africa, always winning the confidence of those he met, always giving encouragement, always inspiring high and low, strong and weak, ruler and ruled." These words of its Chairman are echoed by other members of the Commission. Most notable is the fact that never during all the long months in which Dr. Aggrey received the acclamations of African people and the confidence of white men, did he play off one group against another or stand among the Commission as an individual with resources and ends of his own. Loyalty and simplicity kept him in an all-round partnership of fellowship and truth.

What next? An experience so great pointed to some new service in Africa. Further and strenuous study which he had undertaken at Columbia University between the two Commission visits pointed to educational work. For the

degree of Doctor of Philosophy all examinations
had been passed with high credit, as Professor
Giddings wrote; it only remained to submit the
required thesis. He had not long to wait. A
clear call to notable service for God and for
Africa came.

Part Two. 1924-1927

GREAT plans were in progress during 1926 on
the western side of Africa. While the second
Educational Commission was visiting the east
and the south, Sir Gordon Guggisberg, Governor
of the Gold Coast, who had been closely in touch
with the first Commission in 1920-21 and had
made friends with its African member, had in
mind a new secondary school at Accra. But it
was wisely decided to secure a rural rather than
an urban site. A waterless uncultivated hill was
chosen, high and healthy, covered with grass and
scrub and about eight miles inland from Accra.
Here an area of four square miles was acquired
by government, giving ample room for expansion. Gradually plans for the Accra Secondary
School grew into plans for Achimota College,
and in April 1924 the governor laid the
foundation stone.

When Dr. Aggrey returned to England from Africa in the summer of 1924 the British Colonial Office were selecting a staff for Achimota. Principal A. G. Fraser, who had made such a splendid success of Trinity College, Kandy, Ceylon, was urged to give himself to shaping the new institution. The governor of the Gold Coast and Principal Fraser proposed Dr. Aggrey as a member of the staff; the Colonial Office wisely and cordially offered an appointment; Dr. Aggrey agreed to go.

"He it was," wrote Principal Fraser, "who persuaded me to go out to Achimota. But for him I would not have gone, for he knew the people and could help me to know them, and no one else could have done that. So I made his coming with me one of my conditions for acceptance of that work. He came at what was at first a pecuniary sacrifice. Never had a man a more loyal fellow-worker, and he was invaluable in the special work he had to do."

Gradually the great site at Achimota was fenced, sections cleared, roads made, plans marked out, pipe water laid on, electric light and power provided. A sewage farm, a cattle farm, a vegetable garden, came into being; for games two large oval cricket grounds, five football and three hockey grounds, twelve tennis courts were laid out; there was ample room for more. Buildings rose rapidly and are rising still. The site was divided between the school and the college—both called after the Prince of Wales—with the hospital lying between. Achimota is planned to accommodate over one thousand persons, seven hundred and seventy being students, of whom about one-third will be in the school and two-thirds in the college. The maximum number will not in either case be reached for several years.

The whole scheme of Achimota attracts by its flexible completeness. In the school there will be kindergarten for boys and girls, lower primary for girls and boys up to eight, and an upper primary for girls only. In the college the boys will have their upper primary and a secondary school and university college, the two latter being open to girls also. Both school and college are well supplied with classrooms, dining rooms, dormitories and bungalows for staff. There are also engineering workshops and art and science rooms. This is the outline of an experiment which would be noteworthy in the West, let alone in an African colony.

But it was the Achimota ideal, not its scale

and its equipment, which won Dr. Aggrey to its service.

"The Achimota tradition, if one may use that word of this new college," he said to a friend, "is that of service for country; cooperation irrespective of color; and education of head, hand and heart. Our aim is to take all the best in African culture and combine it with the best in the culture of the West. This means that we give much attention to indigenous art, to crafts and to African music. Even such an art as that of the drum language, a wonderful branch of African culture, will, I hope, be studied. I have recently been specially occupied in giving courses to teachers in West African history. Some of the staff have been traveling over the country obtaining material on this subject and also on geography. Textbooks and a syllabus for different standards are being gradually drawn up to instruct the children in ancient Native rights in the village community, in the home, in training for trades, and in relation to the clan, the state, law, and social customs."

In the midst of this great organization of Achimota there was no more strenuous worker than Dr. Aggrey himself. It was his special function to interpret the aim and purpose of the college to the peoples of the Gold Coast. To this he gave himself with passionate energy and found joy in his costly task.

"His house was next to mine," writes the acting principal of Achimota. "I know the life he lived. Up early, reading and writing through half the night, eating at the longest intervals, eating almost nothing even then; always working, never resting, constantly interrupted, he filled his crowded days with labor. And four times a month he would be away on long journeys to distant places where two or three days would be spent, with every moment between exhausting speeches given to more exhausting talk."

Another colleague says, "If Mr. Fraser was the captain of the ship, Dr. Aggrey was the pilot who helped to guide it through difficult waters." His work was not unnoticed by the colonial authorities. Sir Gordon Guggisberg shows that every detail was known to him:

"Aggrey's task was in his mind day and night. No trouble was too great for him, no help that he could give was ever refused. Constant traveling, constant public speaking, long and interminable arguments with those whom he believed to be on the wrong path, long letters to those whom he could not reach, hours of teaching the young Africans in the schools, such were Aggrey's days in the Gold Coast. Only a real faith that lifted him above himself could have sustained him in the last three years, and he had that faith, the real faith of a real Christian."

Dr. Aggrey found special joy in the relation which began to spring up between the chiefs and Achimota. He noted the day when they first spoke of it as "our college." "The interest has been extraordinary as I have gone about," he said. "The chiefs call in the people from miles round to hear about the college. In one town they built a special great roofed hall in the market-place, as they had no place large enough to hold the people. After they had heard about Achimota they adopted me as a son of the town. When I had finished speaking, it rained. The chief said, 'This is God's rain to make Dr. Aggrey's seeds grow.' He also invited his people who could not give money to come and break rocks to enlarge the local school. After this the chief called a meeting of leading men to discuss education. It lasted from noon to two a.m."

The one shadow which darkened his vivid life at Achimota was the suspension of those intimate home relations so peculiarly dear to him. His wife indeed joined him on the Gold Coast before his house at Achimota was built; she won the friendship of his people and especially of the chiefs. But health failed her and she had to return to America, leaving him behind.

In the summer of 1927 leave of absence was given that he might complete the thesis for his Columbia degree and visit his home at Salisbury, North Carolina, where a little son had been born to him. A few strenuous, happy weeks were spent in England en route. His face was lighted with remembrance not only of friends but even of casual acquaintances; he dropped naturally, with mingled reticence and brilliance, into committee work, and displayed an almost uncanny knowledge of current events and British life. Radiant with joy at his homegoing, he talked of the prowess of the baby boy, to whom he was bringing from a West Coast chief some water from the sacred spring Kakawa in which his own infant head had been bathed.

Within a few hours of reaching England he was at work upon his book. Thoughts which fell over each other as they struggled for utterance were brought into order; a preliminary scheme was made. The experience of his life in three continents was to enrich that book; into it was to be garnered all the truth he saw; it was to be his greatest essay at interpreting white rulers and African races to each other. The moment the meetings of the Colonial Conference were over and Sir Gordon Guggisberg, whose tenure of office on the Gold Coast had ended, was free, the administrator and the African seer met to discuss the draft. It was an association unique in interest.

Two months Dr. Aggrey proposed to spend in America: in his home circle at Salisbury, with friends here and there, and at work on his book amid the rich and familiar resources of Columbia University. In September he would come back to London to finish his book in the house of a friend. November was to see him back in Achimota, in time for the conference of leaders with the African chiefs before the term began.

Eager and full of vital purpose he sailed for New York, laden with official records of the Gold Coast. A fortnight at Salisbury in his beloved house in the longed-for company of wife and children and the baby; then back to kindly friends and keen study in New York. A fortnight later, in a moment, deadly disease was upon him, and after one day's illness he died.

In those summer days of July and August the news of his death passed throughout the world. In the three continents where he had stood exponent of the gifts of Christian Africa thousands mourned him, many with profound affection and esteem. They recalled his sayings and doings; stories of him were repeated from mouth to mouth. Somehow, in face of his abounding vital energy, it came as an astounding shock that he should be holden of death.

In New York a great company met to give thanks for his splendid service; at Salisbury wife and children and intimate friends gathered round his grave. At Achimota the new Governor, Sir Ransford Slater, summoned officials and Native peoples to a solemn memorial service in which he himself took part; the aged mother and the sister of Dr. Aggrey were there. Like services were held in Accra, in Cape Coast, and in Kumasi. In London the African residents met to honor his memory as they had met to bid him Godspeed. The press in all three continents and notably in Great Britain and West Africa gave record of his career. A modern statesman of any race would be honored by the tributes which this son of Africa received.

Some of those who wrote of him go far deeper

than eulogy; they set the man as they knew him
livingly before our eyes. Here, in a few simple
paragraphs, Principal Fraser pictures his friend:

I knew Aggrey better than most men, probably.
For in the first year of our work in the Gold Coast the
staff were all located in one house, and some of us
had to sleep two in a room. Aggrey and myself
shared a room for a considerable time. He was a delightful man to live with, full of humor, never taking
offence, always looking on the bright side of things.
He was devoted to his people and country and was
unsparing of himself. He was equally ready to spend
his time and labor over the poorest as over the most
powerful, and was as accessible to them.

The humor with which he took rebuffs was quite
deliberate and meant great self-mastery. But the
mastery was so complete that it appeared easy not
only to others but to himself. Once, for instance,
he was traveling, the only African on board a
steamer. So he was placed at a table by himself, and
no others sat with him. An intensely sociable man,
he was cut off from all other passengers. Gradually,
however, some passengers got to talk to him, and one
asked him if he did not resent having to take his meals
in solitary state. "No," he said, "that's where I laugh.
You people have one steward to six of you. I have
a steward all to myself."

He was almost an ascetic. He ate only a light
breakfast, and would often eat no more until the
next breakfast. But he was no ascetic in spirit. He

rigorously kept down his appetites, for he felt that indulgence in them had been the bane of his country-men.

He was one of the purest men I have ever met. And he was a great human being. He was a friend to men and interested in all of them, and always kindly.

I have had many good things in life, but one of the best is having been allowed to know Aggrey intimately and well.

Canon Phelps Stokes, in the testimony which he bore at the New York memorial service, affirmed also what Principal Fraser wrote:

In my long acquaintance with Dr. Aggrey I have never heard him say an impure thing, nor known him to act from anything except the highest motives. His was a clean and an unsullied purpose. . . . His real humility has been most marked wherever he has been during the past five years in Africa. . . . Praise in public and in private did not turn his head, for he was a humble servant of his Master.

Again, one of the leading officials in the British Colonial Office wrote, a few days after Dr. Aggrey's death:

It will not be on account of his exceptional personal achievement or of his outstanding contribution to the educational progress of Africa that he will be chiefly remembered by his many friends. What will be remembered by them will be his most lovable personality. Endowed with great gifts, he was of all men most humble. He possessed in a peculiar degree that simple Christianity which was the guiding impulse of his life.

This is strikingly borne out by what Dr. Aggrey wrote to an intimate friend of his only six weeks before his death:

"The one thing I am most proud of is my conversion to Christianity and the great help I daily have from communion with the Father by his Son and through the Spirit. God and I are on good terms. He understands me and makes me work hard every day to reach his standard for me, because, wonderful to relate, he has such confidence in me. I pray in deep humility that I may never disappoint him."

Sir Gordon Guggisberg thus sums up the character of the man whom he termed his friend:

In the passing over of Aggrey, Africa has lost one of her greatest sons. For the essence of Aggrey was that he was an African imbued with the ancient customs and traditions of his people, his knowledge of the way in which they thought being undisturbed by his Western education or his long sojourn and brilliant scholastic career in the United States of America.

But his deep affection for his people and their customs never blinded him for a moment to the fact that changes must come, conditions and manner of life and thought must alter, if his beloved Africans were to keep pace with modern civilization in a continually advancing world.

At the same time, equally and very keenly, he felt that any changes that came to his people must not alter their personality, their spirit, their character, as Africans. That was his constant anxiety: how to give them the opportunities for acquiring all the learning, all the knowledge of arts and crafts, all the mental poise and character, that centuries of slow progress have given to the civilized nations of the world, and yet how to ensure that they retain the spirit of their ancestors.

It was on this task, brimful of energy, overflowing in long and impassioned speeches, that he started in the Phelps-Stokes Commission that visited Africa in 1921. It was this task he continued when he came to Achimota as a simple master in 1924. It was for this task—for "my people who want me"—that he refused high advancement and a considerably greater salary in an American University.

In one way Aggrey was so particularly valuable to the world that he is at present irreplacable; he was a magnificent link between black and white. Who that heard him will forget his simile of the black and white keys of the piano both being necessary for melody? Or his stories of the thoughtless and often overbearing treatment which he himself had received in various parts of the world from the white man, and of the cheerful jests with which he met this treatment, itself—as he termed it—merely a passing incident in the evolution of his race?

Aggrey indeed was the finest interpreter which the present century has produced of the white man to the black, of the black man to the white. To neither, in his private conversation, was he sparing in his criticism of their failings; but it was kindly criticism, for, as he once said, the failings were not personal but inherent in the system which has hitherto dominated the relations of black and white.

I have written of my friend Aggrey as I found the man, found him in many long and very personal talks with him, found him in his work. Of all the men I know, Aggrey was most prepared to cross the great river; he would not grieve except for leaving his wife and children and his unfinished task. There are others to come. May his example stimulate them. May we have more Aggreys in our great continent of Africa.

And so, old friend, rest in peace. You have laid the foundations for the road along which your beloved Africans are marching.

The Legislative Council of the Gold Coast Colony, at its meeting at Accra in September, 1927, by a standing vote, placed on record "its sense of the great loss to the cause of education, social service, and moral progress sustained through Dr. Aggrey's death." The new governor told the Council that the outgoing governor, in giving him advice on many subjects, had said of Dr. Aggrey, "You may absolutely trust him."

X. MEN OF AFFAIRS

THE four chapters which follow, unlike those which precede them, contain several outline sketches instead of single studies worked out at more length. This is designed to provide the fullest possible range of evidence as to African characteristics and capacity. Some of these Africans are widely known; others are eminent only in one locality. We begin with a group of those who in one way or another have been men of affairs.

℣ EDWARD WILMOT BLYDEN, *Scholar and Diplomat*

Edward Wilmot Blyden was born in 1832 on the Island of Saint Thomas, then one of the Danish possessions in the West Indies. In 1851 he came to Liberia in search of education. Henceforth until his death in 1912 he devoted himself to the country of his adoption and to the interests of the African race. He became a Liberian subject and remained one all his life. He was one of the most distinguished sons of Africa.

The young man studied first at the Institute of the Presbyterian Board of Missions in Monrovia, of which he later on became principal, and then at Liberia College, where he was afterwards a leading professor. He owed to subsequent study in American colleges his M.A. and LL.D. degrees. He was at one time government Director of Mohammedan Education in Sierra Leone.

Under the Liberian government he held many offices of responsibility. When Sir Havelock Ellis, as British plenipotentiary, was carrying on the boundary negotiations between Great Britain and Liberia in 1871, he dealt with him as Minister of the Interior. Dr. Blyden was also at various times Secretary of State, Vice-President of Liberia, and Liberian Minister Plenipotentiary at the Court of St. James's. He made many friends in England and was an honorary member of the Athenæum Club.

He was a man of great learning, well versed, as Sir Harry Johnston says, in Greek and Latin; he also knew several European languages. He was a brilliant Arabic scholar. He had wide relations with learned and philanthropic societies: he was a Fellow of the American Philological Society, and a vice-president of the American

Colonization Society so closely concerned in the welfare of Liberia; he was a vice-president of the African Society (London) and corresponding and honorary member of the Society of Science and Letters in Bengal.

Dr. Blyden left a number of excellent lectures in pamphlet form, and a notable book called *Christianity, Islam, and the Negro Race*. Though illuminating in its outlook on the African, the book is open to challenge in its views on Christianity and Islam. Dr. Blyden believed that the African needed a Christian church in which place was found for regulated polygamy, and that Islam was so suited to the African that it offered a half-way house between paganism and the Christian faith. On both points he would have been at issue with Dr. Aggrey, who repudiated with indignation the offer of Islam as even a temporary substitute for Christianity—"The African needs the best." And, with Khama, Dr. Aggrey held strongly that monogamy was possible for the African and offered him the only true basis of life.

Is it because of his learning that Dr. Blyden— the only man not born in Africa who finds place in these pages—has been included here? Not so. His peculiar significance lies in his attitude

towards the aboriginal peoples whom he held
to be "the life and backbone of the country."
"The race," he said, "in its integrity is in the interior. We must learn to occupy the standpoint
of our aboriginal brother, and to believe that in
his own place there is no man better than he or
equal to him." Too often these unlettered tribes
have been looked down on by the Afro-Ameri-
can emigrants to Liberia who are mainly the governing class. It is interesting to compare Dr.
Blyden's utterances with the principles laid
down in the latest book on Liberia.[1] The agreement is complete.

Here are other words of gold which he spoke:

Every race, every state, which is to lead a life of
its own, has a constitution existing in the order of
things, written "in the manuscripts of God." It
cannot be read at once and adopted by sudden enact-
ment. It comes to the knowledge of the people by
slow degrees, by years and years of experiment and
experience. . . . I smile when I hear some Liberians
express the apprehension that if they were to conform to the laws of Africa—the constitution established by Nature—they would be internationally
ostracized. Why, I am sure that our international
status would be immensely advanced and our international relations strengthened. England, France,

[1] *Liberia, Old and New*, by James L. Sibley and Diedrich Westermann;
Doubleday, Doran & Co., New York, 1928.

Germany, and the United States would be too pleased to welcome a new plant, if genuine, in the flora of the nations.   At any rate, it is better to be censured or even ridiculed for being yourself than applauded for trying to be someone else.

▰ JOHN MENSAH SARBAH, *Lawyer and Author*

In the Gold Coast section of any public library, the index of the best works by administrators, travelers or anthropologists has the entry, "Sarbah, J. M."   On turning up the entry a reference is given to a book.   It is clear that J. M. Sarbah has written something authoritative.   Curiosity is stirred as to the author.

Among the group of interesting men whom Dr. Aggrey's father counted as intimate friends was Captain John Sarbah, Native member of the Legislative Council of the Gold Coast colony.   He was in command of the Gold Coast Rifle Corps during the Ashanti Expedition of 1873-75.   He was one of the leading merchants of Cape Coast Castle and had several branch businesses.   He was a man universally respected and was a prominent office-holder in the Wesleyan church.   His wife, like himself, was of high Native rank.   His son, John Mensah Sarbah, describes him thus: "A merchant enterpris-

ing and honorable, a statesman loyal and fearless, a patriot chivalrous and true, a parent pious
and most affectionate."

His son, whose name haunts the indices of
books about the Gold Coast, was born in 1863,
educated first at the Wesleyan School in Cape
Coast Castle, and then at Wesley College, Taunton, England. In later years he founded at
Taunton, in appreciation of help given there, a
small scholarship, open to white as well as black.
He took up the study of law and was called to
the bar at Lincoln's Inn, London. On returning to the Gold Coast he began to practise in the
local courts. Success was assured from the first.
His ability and the quiet effective way in which
he handled cases appealed alike to clients and to
the bench. By degrees he gained an unusual
knowledge of Native law and custom, both in its
application and interpretation.

In the Gold Coast courts when cases arose between Natives, especially cases concerning land
and inheritance, adjudication had to be in accordance with Native customary law. Many of
the Native chiefs had considerable knowledge
and experience, and their advice was frequently
sought. But no fully qualified member of the
legal profession had made a study of the sub-

ject, or classified the principles which underlay Native law.

This was the task to which John Mensah Sarbah addressed himself. Both as a lawyer and as an African the subject was grateful to him. As he practised in the courts he kept careful records. He was given access to many official documents, and gradually accumulated material which he shaped into a book. *Fanti Customary Laws* was published in 1897; the London *Times* called attention to it in an appreciative review. The book at once found place in all important libraries and is consulted as an authority still.

A distinguished career was open before this African lawyer, still in middle life. Like his father he became a member of the Legislative Council. The government valued his guidance in all matters pertaining to Native law and custom; he held the respect of his own people through the care with which he represented their views. He was made a Companion of the Order of St. Michael and St. George (C.M.G.) in 1903. In December 1910 after a brief illness he died.

Like Dr. Blyden, the Hon. J. M. Sarbah held that law, whether foreign or Native, was a reflection of natural character and arose out of the circumstances of life. He felt that the preservation of Native law was essential for the welfare of the people, but in conserving it he saw that new conditions made some changes natural and right. He was a man who always thought before he took action. He was singularly fitted to be a link between the executive government and his fellow-countrymen. He believed in the capacity of the African for administrative work; he was active in the cause of higher education and sought to develop it on Native lines; bearing in mind that the people of the Gold Coast were by descent and occupation farmers, he furthered the advance of agriculture. It is good to realize how many of the recent developments in the Gold Coast—administrative, educational and agricultural—have been in the direction of his desires.

¶ JOHN TENGO JABAVU, *Editor and Patriot*

John Tengo Jabavu, born in January 1859, near Fort Beaufort in Cape Province, has many claims to a place among African men of affairs. He is admittedly one of the outstanding representatives of the Christian Bantu who have served South Africa.

Take the story of his education. From the day when he combined his first lessons with his

duties as a little herdboy on the hillsides, up to
his matriculation at Cape University—the second African to pass that test—his education is
one long record of his parents' sacrifice and his
own indomitable industry. Mary Mpinde, his
mother, earned money as a laundress to pay for
her boys at school.

Take his literary work. He learned to be a
printer by putting in a day's work in a newspaper office before breakfast, and then, hastily
cleansed from printer's ink, did his full day's
teaching in school. He became editor of the
Lovedale paper *Isigidimi*, and later was enabled
to found the *Imvo*, an important Native newspaper published in English and in Kafir, which
he carried on till his death.

Take his work for the cause of Native education. He knew by his own experience as a
teacher what education could effect. In his
happy home he and Elda, his musically gifted
wife, had to face the education of their boys.
By obstacles placed in the way of his son, he
proved that in South Africa the road to higher
education was not clear. In the pages of *Imvo*
he was an advocate, sometimes a vehement one,
of the removal of all that barred the advance of
his people to knowledge. He gave himself to

long-continued, strenuous and successful work in connection with the founding of the South African Native College at Fort Hare, Cape Province, on the staff of which his son, Professor D. D. T. Jabavu, now holds an honored place. So active was he in promoting plans for this great enterprise that the Natives used to speak of the new college as *I Koleji yika Jabavu,* Jabavu's College. He served on the Provincial Education Commission on Native Education in 1920, shortly before his death, being one of the first four Natives appointed on any government commission.

Take his political career. From the early days when he was the principal Native supporter of Mr. (afterwards Sir James) Rose-Innes, the future Chief Justice of the Union of South Africa, Mr. Tengo Jabavu took a fearless and clean-handed part in political affairs. He was loyal to his own people and did not scruple to fight for their rights. But he was an intelligent and thoughtful student of politics and could weigh issues which many of his fellow-countrymen failed to perceive. He set himself to do an educative work among the Native electorate of Cape Province. Like Dr. Aggrey, who went to see him in South Africa and spoke of him as "a man of vision," he acted as interpreter between white and black. He believed the races were meant to help and supplement one another.

Once he lost the confidence of the Natives by supporting a parliamentary bill which they vigorously, and probably with justice, opposed. He was too downright to know how to conciliate critics and never fully gained the leadership of his people again. But to the last day of his life he held the confidence of the responsible white officials. They heard him with respect even if they differed from his views. They knew he served no private ends. The Prime Minister of the Union of South Africa wrote after his death: "The name of Tengo Jabavu is a household word throughout South Africa. . . . The sanity of his outlook and integrity of his character commanded respect. His ability as a man and his skill as a journalist compelled admiration."

Mr. R. W. Rose-Innes of King Williamstown, brother of the man at whose side Jabavu began his political work and one of the two friends whose financial support made possible the founding of *Imvo*, bore this testimony based on the friendship of many years:

"Mr. Jabavu was a man of high character, of wide influence and of great ability. He was a

keen politician. He was a man who for many
years exercised power throughout the Union of
South Africa. It will be a matter of great difficulty to replace Mr. Jabavu in the editorship of
Imvo as the wise, moderate, far-seeing coun-
sellor of his fellow-countrymen, on the Council
of the South African Native College, and in the
offices which he filled from youth upward in
the Wesleyan church. Courteous always; tem-
perate in the expression of his views and sympa-
thies, which he tenaciously held to the last; bold
and courageous where boldness and courage were
needed; self-effacing and yet self-respecting;
modest and yet outspoken—his death at sixty-
two years of age will be mourned by many. . . .
A long and faithful discharge of duty is a fine
memorial."

KANJUNDU, *Chief near Bihé, Angola*

The open-eyed student of African life finds
men of affairs not only amongst highly educated Africans but also among lesser chiefs,
who, emerging from unfavorable surroundings
through steady growth in character, make a
good thing of life for their people and for themselves. Such a man was Kanjundu, chief of
Chiyuka, a village near Bihé in Angola, West

Central Africa. His story is gathered from fragmentary material which builds up into picturesque form.

First there emerges a strong, passionate man, tall, erect and slender, irritated by ill-health, renowned for harshness and cruelty to his slaves and his people, armed with a huge hippotamus-hide whip wherewith floggings are frequently given. He has spirit-houses and idols and endless weird fetishes of bones and turtle shells, bought at great cost by exchange of bales of cloth and powder and pigs and oxen and slaves. When illness is on him he sits on a sacred mat while incantations and exorcisms are performed over him.

A little later we see that he has come to the mission station in search of health. Soon he stays there in search of teaching. At morning prayers he is the first arrival. He wants to learn to read and write. He realizes that he will have to face the question of his many wives. He tears down the spirit-houses, he destroys the heathen emblems for which he expended so much. Still hesitating between the old way and the new, he leads a caravan from Bihé to the Barotse Valley to trade. And lo! it has become a Christian embassy. Two mission helpers go to teach the young men. Some of the lads are already Christian. The chief finds himself opposing beer and strong drink. He will not accept presents of liquor, even when tempted with five bottles, each containing a different kind. He is offering Christian medicine in place of fetich. His temper, too, is better than on previous trips.

He comes back resolved to be a Christian. In a great speech to his people he renounces the old way in which he had believed from childhood, and is "determined to follow Jesus Christ." As a missionary writes, "When he was converted it was literally coming into the Kingdom of Heaven like a little child. He at once freed his slaves, over a hundred in number, providing each one with a little home. He endeavored to atone for his past harshness by treating each one as he would his child. From among his wives he selected one as his lawful partner and provided justly for the rest."

The new life begins to spread. But Kanjundu, like Khama, has the drink trade to fight. A false accusation is brought against him by a discomfited trader who declares the chief has burnt down his store. Kanjundu is dragged to a miserable prison and kept there for two years in the hope that he will confess a deed he never did. All the time his faithful people visit him with food and words of cheer. When release comes he gets an ovation which startles the whole countryside. Africans appreciate a good chief when he comes their way.

Now at last, in the sphere of his chieftainship, Kanjundu is free to translate his faith into works. The great whip hangs unused on his wall. He governs and governs well, but by love instead of fear. Improvements appear in his village. Streets are laid out, yards are kept cleaner, those who will not conform to sanitary regulations are obliged to live apart. The chief himself has a three-roomed house, fresh and clean and attractive, with windows, and some furniture, and pictures of Scripture scenes on the walls. He has become more refined and gentle in his ways. He readily shares a family meal in a missionary home. He does not rest until every village within his influence has all its children in school. In his own village he has a church and a school large enough for a mission station. He is an elder of the church and an acceptable preacher. The people welcome him as if he were a white missionary. The Portuguese residents have been won to believe in his sincerity and admit that his influence in the country is of great value. The prominent Portuguese trader who has lived in his village for years backs Kanjundu against all the other chiefs for solid worth.

This is the story, in mere outline, of Chief Soma Kanjundu up to October 1914, when the good man died. The hippotamus-hide whip which he used to ply may be seen in the offices of the American Board in Boston. His story can be heard there at first hand from those who knew him and are able to vouch for the manner of man he was.

℉ DAVID LIVINGSTONE'S SERVANTS

There is no more familiar story in the annals of Africa than that of the little group of faithful servants who bore the body of their great dead master to the coast. Sermons without number have been preached on that text of faithful devotion. But to the revelation of other aspects of African character in that story little attention has been paid. Here follows a brief study of Livingstone's servants as men of affairs.

The great explorer had come to the end of his third journey. His heroic effort, made after Stanley left him, to wrest from Central Africa more secrets of its lakes and rivers, had failed. He was borne in weakness and suffering to Chi-

tambo's village in Ilala.   In the morning of May
1, 1873, Majwara, the faithful lad who was with
him, found him kneeling by his bedside dead.

We turn from the greatest of the men who
have lived and died for Africa to the little
leaderless group who stand sorrowful and dis-
mayed.   On that May Day, when merry folk
were dancing on village greens in England, these
Africans were faced by a challenge impossibly
great.   The desperate strain of those weeks of
nightmare struggle through the spongy marshes
of Lake Bangweolo, carrying a dying man, were
easy compared with what they saw ahead.   From
their own close intercourse with him, and from
Stanley's coming and his words, they knew that
their dead master was honored by all the world.
They could not leave him in the wilds alone.
It was for them to take his wasted work-worn
body to his own kin and country, whatever the
cost.   It was an utterly African decision.

Look well at the little group.   There are the
five whom Stanley has immortalized for their
fidelity: Susi, from Shupanga on the Zambesi, first a wood-cutter on Livingstone's little
steamer the *Pioneer,* then by degrees promoted
to be headman of all the followers, a quick, intelligent man, his thin and careworn face

marked a little by smallpox; Chuma of the Yao tribe, a special friend of Susi's, a smooth-faced man, lighter in color, vivacious in his ways, rescued from slavery long before by Bishop Mackenzie and Livingstone, and a student in the mission for three years (it was Chuma who took the adventurous voyage across the Indian Ocean when Livingstone navigated the little *Lady Nyassa* to Bombay); Amoda, another Shupanga man who began as a wood-cutter like Susi (he had with him Halima his wife who acted as cook); Mabruki and Gardner, two boys rescued after capture and brought up at the home for freed slaves at Nasik in western India—these were Stanley's five. There stands out also Jacob Wainwright, another African trained at Nasik. It fell to him to be one of the pall-bearers when Westminster Abbey received the body of Livingstone among its honored dead.

The details of that ten months' march to the coast might well fill many pages.

With wisdom and resourcefulness the little party took up their task. Chitambo the chief proved worthy of the confidence which after a moment's hesitation they gave him. In some new huts, which they built outside the village and guarded night and day, the body was rev-

erently prepared for transport to the coast.
They had so little knowledge of what to do, and
made that little effect so much. The heart
which beat to the last for Africa was, with a
singular touch of inspiration, buried beneath a
mvula tree. The journey led often through unknown country, across rivers, over a mountain
range, through forests and plains. All chiefs
were not as Chitambo. The bearers were often
excluded from villages and mulcted heavily of
their scanty goods. Once they were involved in
actual warfare when Amoda's carelessly handled
musket discharged itself among village people.

When the wilder country had been traversed
a new danger arose. The news of their march
preceded them—in Africa it is always so. Suspicion as to the burden they bore so tenderly
began to turn into certainty. The village chiefs
became afraid. The passing of a body through
their territory might bring ill-luck. It began to
be said that the party should be driven back to
Unyanyembe to lay the dead man there. The
"men of affairs" tried persuasion and gifts as
long as they had wherewith to give. But still
the danger grew. So they laid a new plan. Outside a village, under a watchful guard, a faggot
of mapira stalks was made to look like a body,

draped in cotton and slung on long poles. Then the body was swathed to look like a bale.

Towards evening some of the porters set off in full view of the village along the path leading back to Unyanyembe, bearing the long bundle on their shoulders. When well out of sight in the bush they leaped off the path to leave no trace of their footsteps, broke up the bundle, and hid the pole and the mapira stalks in the undergrowth. Then one by one they made their way to the camp outside the unsuspecting village and set forward next day, guarding the bale which held their sacred trust.

All this and much more can be read in the appendix to Livingstone's last journal, and in the records of his life. One matter and one only concerns us here: Did these simple Africans show qualities which rank high among the families of mankind? How should we appraise them if they were "hundred-per-cent Americans" or "British-born"?

XI. EVANGELISTS, PASTORS, TEACHERS

THE preceding chapters have offered evidence that Africans, non-Christian or Christian, are not a feeble folk. Here we add testimony as to some of the rank and file of that great body of Christian Africans who are employed by churches and missions to spread the gospel. There are, according to the latest computation, about thirty-seven thousand working in relation with Protestant missions, besides those in the service of the Roman Catholic church.[1] In addition, of course, there is the part-time voluntary Christian work of African men and women, as varied and often as devoted as that given in churches in the West.

Every country having Christian missions in Africa is continually recording the capacity, devotion, and spiritual reality of many African colleagues—none more so than the United States and Canada. Take what North American mission board you will, read its books and its peri-

[1] Statistical tables for Africa in the World Missionary Atlas for 1925 show a native staff of about 16,000 in British missions, about 9,000 in American missions, and nearly 6,000 in South African agencies.

odicals, question its missionaries, and a wealth of
new evidence will be tapped. The varied information gathered for the 1928 jubilee of Congo
missions, and the newer literature produced by
the Missionary Education Movement, raise a
peak above even the high level of the past. To
these records accessible directly to American
readers we add five taken from the sphere of
English, German, French and Swiss missions in
Africa, and the story of a great evangelistic work
purely spontaneous and African in origin.

⧉ *The Call of the Congo Forest:* APOLO KIVUBULAYA *at Work*

On a shoulder of snow-crowned Ruwenzori
an African stood in the year 1896. Behind him,
eastward and about two hundred miles away, lay
Uganda whence he had come, commissioned by
the church as an evangelist to Toro.

When he had reached Toro, and looked at the
great mountain which no foot of gospel messenger had crossed, his pioneer spirit had risen
within him; he felt that at least he must see
what was lying on the other side. They had told
him down in Toro that evil befell those who
climbed the mountain. But fear had no hold
upon this man, and up he went until he stood

upon the mighty shoulder, a new world opening to his view.

Below him the hills dropped downward, fold after fold, to the plain where the Semliki River wound its way in glittering beauty. Dark tongues of acacia bush broke the green and merged at length in the vast black Congo forest filling the westward horizon. There the pygmies dwelt. To the north, melting into the distance, the waters of the great Lake Albert Edward shimmered in a pearly haze; southward the shoulder of the mountain sloped boldly, streaked with rushing waters from the snow.

The steps of this pioneer, Apolo Kivubulaya, turned backward to Toro, but his heart had gone out forever to the forest and the plain that he had seen from the peak. Ere long he was settled in Mboga, a pleasant village on a range of beautiful hills eighteen miles beyond the Semliki River and not far from the forest glades. He had small equipment for founding a mission in virgin soil. In his early days he had met with Alexander Mackay. Boylike, his enthusiasm fixed on the stranger—"love seemed to shine out of his eyes." He learned a bit here and there, but long years of soldiering in Uganda left him little time for school. At last, away in the bush

and surrounded with enemies, he heard the voice
of Jesus. He became an eager reader of the
Bible, and as soon as possible he was baptized.
On the day when he stood on the shoulder of
Ruwenzori he was just a sturdy, eager, humble,
fearless Christian, with little knowledge and few
mental gifts, but burning to tell others of his
Savior and Lord.

Thousands of people lived in the districts
round Mboga, at the mercy of a chief who could
rule neither his people nor himself. Witchcraft,
drunkenness, immorality and cruelty were rife
in the village itself. Expecting to receive something from him, chief and people welcomed
Apolo at first. But when after two years the
first convert, a poor woman rescued from cruel
treatment, was baptized, trouble began. The
chief and the head witch doctors were furious.
Strange tales were spread as to curses which
would come upon those who were baptized.
Apolo's hut was burned to the ground and he
barely escaped. While it was still smoldering he
began to build again. What was a chief to do
with such a man?

He was ordered to leave the country; he replied that God had sent him and he must stay.
He was beaten severely with a whip of hippo-

potamus hide, and beaten again. But it did not move him at all. He went straight on with his work, teaching the people who gathered round him in the little primitive church. Another beating——the worst and the last. He was left for dead, his body being cast into the bush. Of any life in him, the chief grimly said, the wild beasts would soon make an end.

But Apolo lived. The poor ill-treated woman, the first convert, at her peril sought in the bush for his tormented body and found it lying close to the edge of the great forest on which his love was set. In secrecy and through innumerable difficulties she contrived to move him to a disused hut, tending him for six long weary weeks till life moved in him again. He could soon, she said, make good his escape. That was not to Apolo's mind. Back he went to the church the first Sunday morning he could walk there; boldly beat the drum that called the Christians to worship; sat down in his wonted place; took his Bible and began to teach.

Mboga was stirred to its depths: everyone flocked to see the dead man who had come to life again, foremost among them the startled chief. There was Apolo, kindly and cheery as ever, inviting the chief to stay and listen, that he might learn of Christ. The chief was broken. He knelt to Apolo and asked for forgiveness. He led him by the hand to his house. He declared with weeping that God had spoken to him. After due teaching he was baptized. He became Chief Paul Tabalo—as a persecutor he had truly earned the name of Paul.

Thenceforth the little church became too small for the people. A new one was built by the chief. More teachers came from Toro to help Apolo. Mboga was no longer an outpost but a center from which spread Christian light. The Christians out of their poverty found funds for the support of teachers, and besides that built three churches and schools.

It was in 1896 that Apolo Kivubulaya reached Mboga. He works there still. Having faced dangers and persecutions, he now nears the goal of his undeviating course. Gentle, cheerful, unselfish, sensible, he holds on his way, with his hopes still set on the great reaches between Mboga and the Congo. He has penetrated into the forest. He is well known to the pygmies and their king. He is the first to render any portions of the Bible in their language—his primer was printed by the Bible Society in 1926. He can take a white friend now and then into the dark recesses where strange small men and women are earnestly preparing to be baptized into the name of Christ.

Two Africans are canons of the cathedral on Namirembe hill in Kampala; Apolo Kivubulaya is one of the two. When the great jubilee of the Uganda Mission was held in the summer of 1927, many eyes were turned with interest and affection to the small, active, bright-faced African, bearing his years so lightly, still as eager as a boy. The committee of the Church Missionary Society added his name to the long list of their distinguished vice-presidents. Canon Apolo was pleased but puzzled when the committee's letter was translated to him by a medical missionary visiting Mboga. At last he understood. His eyes filled with tears and his faithful old face beamed as he said, "They do it because they love my people." Then he wrote a letter of thanks, got the missionary to translate it, and "threw it away into the post" with his own hands.

F *Forty Years' Service in Togoland*
DAVID BESA, *Lutheran Pastor*

Quite another type of man is Pastor David Besa of Togoland, whose call was to his own people, whose work lay almost unbrokenly in his native town. Born about 1866, he attended a mission school and at twelve years old was baptized. He went out to make his way in the world as a merchant's assistant. As his Christian life strengthened he became a helper in a Wesleyan mission. Then in 1888, burning with zeal, he joined the North German (Bremen) Mission, which had a station in his native town.

Woe, with a population of about three thousand, is capital of a little state of the same name in Togoland, Its history, checkered by wars and slave-raids, reaches back for centuries. It was not a hopeful field. The people were held in thraldom by a heathen cult of peculiar power. Besa's house was close to the grove in which the secret worship was carried on. He passed it every day. Many of his congregation later told how they had once been devotees of the cult but that under Besa's influence its power crumbled away.

The pastor is full of quaint characteristics and goes his own way. He is not devoid of angles and corners but his absolute devotion softens them all. About his personal appearance, unlike most of the better-educated Africans, he cares not at all. He would prefer to walk barefoot and wear country cloth, but he conforms more or less to the usual garb of a Lutheran pastor. He is likely to preach quite unconscious of the fact that his shoes do not match one another and that his collar is out of place. But his sermon will be full of meat. Those who hear him say, "This man preaches from conviction: he uses no empty words." He is absorbed in Bible study and uses such reference books as he has. He is a man of prayer, and of fasting too; he often abstains from a morning or an evening meal. His home life is attractive and his character is above reproach.

On Sundays Besa is at private prayer at four in the morning. His prayer meeting for women begins at five, that for men an hour later. Morning service is at nine. The small chapel in which he began his ministry has given place to a fine large building in which several hundred can worship. It is a living monument, raised by the gifts of Christians and heathen alike, to the reality of the pastor's work. The congregation is always growing; Besa finds his highest joy in the preparation of new candidates for baptism and confirmation. Three or four times a year the European missionary in his official tour of the district has his heart cheered and strengthened by visiting Besa at his work.

During the dark days of the World War, when Togoland passed from German control into the hands of the Allies, Pastor Besa, in conjunction with a Swiss missionary, was able to continue steadfastly at his post.

▰ FRANCIS, *Evangelist in Basutoland*

Francis, as one of his French missionary friends describes him, is a plump, bright-eyed little man about five feet in stature, with a short, pointed beard and a happy smile revealing very white teeth. He speaks with lively gestures and is seldom still. He lives at Hololo in North Basutoland, high up among the hills.

As a shepherd lad he fell in with one of the great successors of the first "men of prayer" who came to Basutoland (see p. 82). This man, M. Dieterlen, took the boy into his service and found him quick and trustworthy. Gradually the light of Christian truth spread through his whole personality; he entered the Bible School and was trained as an evangelist. The two brief records of his work which are extant are dated 1921 and 1926.

In the first record the visiting missionary, looking out from the round hut, neat and spotless, which is the evangelist's home, sees Francis on the slope of the hillside ringing a small bell with a silvery note to summon the Christians to church. They troop down the hillsides, eager to hear, until the little church is crowded and listeners throng round the window and door.

After service, when Francis and Marguerite his wife have entertained the missionary with simple and gracious hospitality, the great project which fills the evangelist's mind is discussed. He wants to build a church, a proper church, large enough for the people, a worthy place wherein to worship God. Yes, he knew it would be costly; even if he gave up the arched windows on which his heart was set it would cost almost fifteen hundred dollars.

"But, Moneri," he went on, "I have already over six hundred dollars in the bank. I have a quantity of stones ready cut, you shall see them. The people are willing to help. If we get another five hundred dollars—and I think we can do it—we might begin to build at once. Help me to choose the best site."

The missionary knew the money had been raised in shillings and sixpences, mainly from Francis's own scanty store. The faith of his black colleague revived his own. He took courage and enlarged his own hopes for the work of

Christ in the land.   He longed and prayed that
Francis might one day see the church of his
dreams, arched windows and all.

In September 1926 the sixteen-year task of
Francis had its great consummation.   Twenty-
five hundred dollars had been raised to build the
church—no less than seven hundred and fifty
given by white men, Boers and British, as a token
of affectionate esteem for the loyal, humble little
man working so indomitably among them.   The
dignity of his life, the sincerity of his convictions, and his apostolic zeal had won their way.
White men in North Basutoland will stop their
automobiles if they meet Francis on the road and
offer him a lift.   That is not commonly done.
Yet no fellow-evangelist is jealous of Francis; he
is too humble, and he has so bright and gentle a
smile.

There he stands, as he stood in 1921, ringing
his silvery bell, his face radiant with joy.   Down
the hillsides, flooded with the light which follows
rain, with the lovely peaks of the snow-decked
Malouti Mountains cutting the blue of the skies,
stream hundreds of horsemen and footmen in
bright-colored robes.   More than five hundred
horses are clustered near by; over two thousand
people are massed on the grassy ground.   There

are a score of Europeans, at least. In the center
of all is the church built by Francis, its door fast
closed. Thrice round the church goes a proces-
sion singing a hymn; at the entrance steps there
is a solemn act of consecration to the service of
God; the key is handed to one chief, who hands
it to another so that no susceptibilities may be
hurt; the door is unlocked; a representative
group enters and deposits the Bible and hymn-
book given by the friends of Francis; an African
pastor offers prayer.

Then the whole great audience forms on the
grassy slope and many speeches are made. One
is by the British Resident at Butha-Buthe, where
Moshesh once lived (see p. 76); in the name of
the British Government he pays a tribute to the
faithfulness of Francis who, by his complete devotion, has gained the love and esteem of all.

Francis in broken words tries to express his
gratitude, and his joy that at last the wish of
his life has been accomplished and the church
of his dreams built. He offers it, and the evangelist's house paid for by his own self-denial, to
the Fathers of France who first sent the gospel
to Basutoland. While the white visitors meet
for tea in the schoolhouse at his invitation, he
distributes meat and flour—much of it presented

for the occasion by still heathen chiefs—to his guests from the mountains and the plains.

Be it remembered that Francis is an African Christian whose intellectual attainments are too slender to qualify him for admission to the pastorate of his church.

¶ CALVIN MATSIVI MAPOPE, *A Thonga Tale*

Scene I. A group of Thonga goatherds, wild, bright lads, eating their midday meal in the bush. After scanty breakfasts in the early morning they drove their restless flocks to pasture; now, having raided the neighbors' fields for maize and sweet potatoes, the boys stay their hunger as they talk. There is excitement today, for one of their number has been to Valdezia and heard the newly come missionaries speak. His version of their teaching is criticized with laughter; it does not fit in with the traditions of the tribe; those, as everyone knows, are correct. One small pair of ears is pricked to listen. Eleven-year-old Matsivi, son of Mapope the village chief, makes up his resolute little mind that he will certainly hear those white men and judge for himself.

Scene II. A few months later. Two little culprits sit facing the village men. At them is pointed the accusing finger of the chief. He is informed that they, his small sons, have been many times to Valdezia to hear the missionaries speak. It is well known that those who listen become fools. A stop must be put to such doings. Public prohibition is laid on the boys; they will be beaten if they disobey.

Scene III. Midnight, chill and dark. Two small boys slip out of a hut and make their way timidly towards the river. They are Matsivi and his younger brother who, like him, has heard with the inward ear. No worthy Thonga boys would continue to visit Valdezia after paternal prohibition. But they cannot, cannot cease to hear those wonderful words. They will run away, independent little fellows that they are, first to the mission station, then, if not welcomed, they will work for the Boers and be free to learn.

It is one thing to be brave by daylight and another at night, when a river has to be forded and there may be the flickering lights which show that death-dealing spirits are about. Hand in hand the little pilgrims make the awesome journey, eyes cast downward lest they see the ghostly lights, ears strained to catch every sound; into the river, across it, up the bank on the other side, and then away to Valdezia.

Scene IV. Nearly fifty years later. The Salle de la Reformation at Geneva is filled with a great audience; numbers have been turned from the doors. It is the jubilee of the Mission Suisse Romande, and Pastor Calvin Matsivi Mapope, delegate representing the Thonga Church at the jubilee, is to speak. It is the intrepid goatherd again. Baptized after a clear conversion at Valdezia in the northern Transvaal, trained first as teacher and then as pastor at Morija in Basutoland, tested in long years of school and pastoral work in rural districts of Portuguese East Africa and in the town of Lourenço Marques, he is a fit representative of the growing African church he has helped to build.

He steps to the front of the platform, his translator by his side. For a moment he gazes on the first large audience of white men he has ever faced. Then with one swift sentence of typical African wit he turns them into friends. "I feel," he says, "like a fly which has fallen into a pot of milk." He speaks simply, clearly, to the point. The chairman rises; "I do not know," he says with a note of hesitation in his voice, "if the gesture would be in order, but—I want to embrace him." In a moment the small African

disappears in the arms of the big Genevese man.
How the audience cheers!

"It was, I think, the first time that many
people had heard an African speak," wrote Dr.
Henri A. Junod,[2] in reference to the ten weeks'
visit of Pastor Calvin Mapope to Switzerland.
"They had a sudden revelation of the extraordinary charm which these races possess: dignity;
self-control touched with spiritual *bonhomie;*
eloquence or at least ease of speech; finesse and
tact amounting sometimes to diplomacy; and an
amazing gift of repartee."

Pastor Mapope was at his best in smaller meetings where questions were asked. He answered
with point and ease. And he never made a mistake. "What do you think of the Christian life
of Switzerland?" he was asked one day. "When
we Africans visit the village of our grandparents
we are advised to put both our hands before our
eyes. I do that," was his quick reply.

Switzerland drew close to Africa in those
jubilee weeks. To dwellers among Swiss mountains and meadows and in towns on the lovely
lakes, Calvin Matsivi Mapope opened a new
world of fellowship with Africans.

[2] Dr. Junod's great book, *The Life of a South African Tribe,* has just
been reissued. It is rich in Thonga lore and missionary experience.

▰ WILLIAM WADÉ HARRIS, *Liberian Prophet*

"A religious event almost incredible in character has upset all preconceived ideas of society among primitive coast Natives." "In the wilderness and in the night, a prophet suddenly appeared." Thus two illustrious Frenchmen, one an administrator, the other a misisonary, refer to the work of the prophet Harris in the contiguous areas of the Gold Coast, the Ivory Coast, and Liberia.

William Wadé Harris belonged by birth to those aborigines of Liberia in whom Dr. E. W. Blyden saw so much hope (see p. 155). He was a Kruman of the Grebo tribe, born near Cape Palmas in Liberia. He was a pupil and afterwards a teacher in the American Methodist school, being baptized at the age of twenty-one. In his early days he went to sea, as Krumen do, and afterwards worked as bricklayer. Being a Grebo he was restless under Americo-Liberian rule; three times he was involved in tribal rebellions—in 1893, 1896 and 1910. Each time he found himself in prison. The third time marked a crisis in his life. In a trance there came to him a call to preach; the Angel Gabriel hailed him as a prophet of God; he was anointed with the spirit; he was told to obey the Bible.

His obedience to this last command has been quite consistent, as he understands it, since 1910. It is the only book he knows; its heroes—David, Daniel, Gabriel—are familiar to him; his personal dependence on it is still complete. A French missionary who recently saw him writes: "His faith is nourished by verses borrowed from the Scriptures. He lives in a supernatural world in which the people, the ideas, the affirmations, the cosmology and the eschatology of the Bible are more real than the things that he sees and hears materially."

The prophet put his commission to preach into force directly he was released from prison. The Liberians did not receive him responsively, and he seems to have made his way to the Gold Coast and begun work there. Thence he passed to the French Ivory Coast about 1913. A religious movement began as he preached, and spread like a flame among the tribes. The government did not interfere with him at first, but became perturbed when a number of teachers poured in to help him from the Gold Coast. Harris was asked to go back across the Liberian frontier; with unfailing dignity, his pilgrim's staff in hand, escorted by the French officials to the frontier, he returned to his native village near Cape Palmas and was lost sight of for years. Over a hundred thousand persons were influenced during the brief period of his teaching, and more than half of this number received baptism from him or from his disciples.

The prophet went away but the movement grew. It is one of the spiritual marvels of the age. Harris did his work outside the sphere of any missionary. He fiercely denounced and completely overthrew fetishism in scores of villages. His converts, blissfully singing in pidgin English Christian hymns which they could not understand, possessed themselves of Bibles—first in English, then, when these were prohibited, in French, neither of which they could read; they built for themselves little churches with no idea of how to carry on worship; they rebuilt them if, by order of the authorities, these were destroyed; deprived of their prophet, they waited patiently for the White Man whom he promised as their leader one day. Judged by common sense and the evidence of history, the "Harris Christians," as they were called, should have relapsed into heathenism or fallen into excesses. Instead they waited on and on, unmoved. Now they are being gathered by the thousand, as rapidly as teachers can be sent, into the ordered Christian church. The magnitude and miracle of the prophet's work can be judged and tested, but it cannot be explained. The sincerity of the man and the sincerity of his converts cannot be called in question.

While those who believed his message are being shepherded and taught, largely by the Wesleyans and also by Roman Catholic missionaries, Harris is living—it is only of late that his retreat has been discovered—in the absolute poverty of a clean-handed man, in a desolate broken-down hut not far from his daughter's home by the seashore of his own village near Cape Palmas. Liberia knows nothing of one of her greatest men. He still carries on, in a quiet patient way, far off from the short scene of his sweeping success, his work of preaching to all who will receive his message. It is the same message which came to him in prison.

There he stands—so a young French missionary saw him with reverent eyes only a few months ago—in his long white robe and turban, with his simple cross of bamboo serving also as a pilgrim's staff, his little Bible, his calabash of water from which now he sprinkles the few as formerly he sprinkled the many of those who come to be baptized. He has no other possessions, save it be the broken bedstead in his hut. Gentle in aspect, vehement in utterance, muscular of frame, in his age and loneliness as fanatical and devoted as in his days of harvest, William Wadé Harris abides, an African who by the mightiness of his own conviction has brought multitudes to the knowledge of the nearness of God.

XII. AMONG THE PROPHETS

THE story of William Wadé Harris leads up to that of other African "prophets," differing widely from him and from one another but all indicating certain characteristics, good and bad, which are central in a study of African life. The stories come first; some comments on their significance follow.

MALAKI *of Uganda*

Eight miles out of Mengo, in a square wood and wattle house thatched with grass, lives Malaki, formerly a certificated teacher in the Uganda church, now the leader of a sect which bears his name. The house may be dirty and unswept, but Malaki, his wife and four children will be found in clean white clothes.

He is a man of about sixty-five years of age, his hair turning gray, his eyes those of an old man. His face in repose is good, with a smile which breaks out all over it. But when he gets on his own particular subject his face grows hard and fanatical, he talks in a loud voice with few pauses; he is evidently ready to die for his convictions—indeed he would welcome the chance. He does not strike one as a man of intellectual power, or of natural force of character, nor has he apparent gifts of leadership. Of course he can read, but his education is slender, for he belongs to the early days in Uganda when provision for training teachers was small. He seems to have some fragmentary acquaintance with church history, for when asked to return his certificate because of the strange doctrines he was teaching, he compared himself to Luther driven out of the church by the Pope.

A senior missionary called at the "prophet's" home a few months ago. Old Malaki, who had long known him, pointed out to him the error of his ways, with dramatic fervor and uplifted hand, crying, "Return unto thy God, for thou hast fallen by thine iniquity." He offered to pray for the conversion of his visitor, that he might fight side by side with Malaki and his followers on behalf of their views.

What is it all about?

In the early days when the Bible was translated into the vernacular, the word charmer, or wizard, was rendered by the common Luganda term. In such passages as *Deuteronomy* 18: 11

the people of Israel are forbidden to allow *basawa* to dwell in the land. Some years later, when medical missionaries arrived in the country, the same familiar word was used for them; indeed there was no choice.[1] Thus it was possible to argue that the forbidden wizards and the mission doctors were one and the same. The unenlightened African, ready to believe in spiritual intervention and to exercise faith, read in the Bible of the healing works of our Lord and noted the absence of any use of medicine in his ministry. Taking literally, as he did, the enactments of the Jewish law, it is quite easy to see how mistaken conclusions were arrived at.

A leading Christian chief, who had always shown a curious mentality, started opposition to the use of medicine in sickness and protested against public prayer for doctors and their work. Under his influence Malaki, who was a small market gardener, began to advocate these views. Soon he believed himself commissioned to baptize the people, on their promise not to touch medicine and on a profession of belief in God and in his son Jesus Christ.

In the Uganda church careful teaching was

[1] Since then the word *doktori* has been imported into the language and is now in common use.

given before baptism; inquirers had to learn to read and to give up heathen ways. The Christian name given only at baptism was always coveted by the people; they welcomed Malaki's shorter and easier way to obtain it. Thousands were baptized by him and his helpers in a few months. Some Christians tempted by polygamy—which Malaki allowed—joined the new sect. At times the movement took awkward forms. The prophet came to one of the church synods and asked permission to speak. This was out of order, so the bishop refused but suggested that after the session was over Malaki might speak to any who remained to hear; he did so, but his audience was small. Malaki and his followers also held abusive meetings and made noisy demonstrations before the hospital and in other parts of Namirembe; these had to be stopped.

The movement, though it still persists, has spent its force. "No longer are there found many going to be baptized this way," wrote a Christian lad. "It is like a stagnant pool of water which has not springs." Malaki and his followers still preach and baptize on lip confession. They have places of worship but few schools. They hold consistently to their beliefs. The Uganda church has never started active propaganda against them. The government does not recognize the sect in its census paper, so their numbers are not known.

Division has crept in among the Malakites. Some want the ancient rites of circumcision; others are against it. Some repudiate the Old Testament and call themselves Jews. Some are returning to the Christian church and after due preparation are being baptized. Many come for treatment to the hospital when ill. At the Mbale dispensary a man presented himself with a bad ulcer. Being a follower of Malaki he was asked why he came. He replied that it was one thing to promise not to take medicine when you wanted "to get your name" (to be baptized), but when pains "began to bite," who would be so foolish as to go without it if it could be had?

Malaki himself, however, is of another mind. Ignorant and fanatical, he is utterly sincere. On the occasion previously mentioned, his missionary visitor, seeing that the old man had fever, tried to open his mind to receive medical treatment. He spoke of God's call to man to be his fellow-worker, and told of the hidden qualities in the chinchona bark which God gave but left man to prepare and use. But Malaki would have none of it. "Is God not strong enough to cure me of my fever if I trust him?" he said.

⚡ ELIJAH II *of Southern Nigeria*

Elijah the Second is introduced in a rather wistful statement written some twelve years ago by the late Dr. Johnson, an African bishop in the Niger River Delta where Samuel Adjai Crowther had made great beginnings long before (see p. 53). Bishop Johnson tells of an upheaval in the Native church.

A young African named Garrick Sokari Braid from Bakana in the New Calabar district had suddenly come into prominence; in barely three months the movement which he started acquired control of a considerable section of the Christian community. He was unable either to read or write, but he was humble and quiet in disposition and zealous and useful in the work of the church. Dreams and visions often came to him and he had power to heal the sick. People came to him from all the Delta and from the Ibo country beyond. At first he worked with his pastor's guidance and encouragement. Then things began to go wrong.

People having called him a prophet, he an-

nounced himself as the second Elijah of whom
Malachi wrote, the prophet who was to come.
His person came to be considered so sacred that
on the march a herald went before him ringing
a bicycle bell, and people knelt while he passed.
Great chiefs, large owners of land, crawled into
his presence and he raised them with his right
hand. The water in which he washed became
sacramental; chiefs and people, rich and poor,
well and ill, scrambled for it and drank it;
women mingled it with clay and used it to adorn
their bodies or to make charms.

Garrick taught, with threats and warnings,
that the use of medical aid or remedies was sin-
ful and would provoke the judgment of God.
He practised healing by faith and prayer and
touch, walking round the sick, laying hands
upon the affected part of their bodies, calling
them to faith in God. He linked sickness and
suffering with sin and insisted on confession. To
confession he added prayer. In the open court
of his large compound at Bakana sick and whole
people might be found praying from ten to sev-
enteen times a day for two or three weeks.
When he came out at intervals to urge them to
perseverance and faith in God, they fell upon
their knees to do him honor and so remained till

he withdrew.   Moses Hart of Bonny, who called
himself "a son of the prophet," used to impose
penance when confession was not readily made.

Heathenism and idolatry were severely denounced by this Elijah.   Chiefs brought out
their old ancestral idols and destroyed them.
Whoso renounced heathenism was ready—the
prophet had it by revelation—to be immediately
baptized.   His disciples went through the villages preaching against idolatry and receiving
idols given up to them; indeed they went
further, for they seized and destroyed idols
which the owners wished to retain.   More than
a hundred of the prophet's preachers were found
guilty of trespass and extortion and sent to
prison for several weeks.   Against strong drink
and the European liquor traffic Elijah the Second
raised an effective voice, reinforced by warnings
and threats.   One man whom he had healed and
warned not to touch strong liquor took some
and died.   He was quoted as a case in point.
Chiefs and Native traders were so influenced
that some would buy no gin at all.   Europeans
who were there to supply them suffered heavy
loss.

It was a time of testing for the Niger Delta
Church.   The congregation at St. Stephen's

Cathedral Church at Bonny were seriously divided, at least three-fourths accepting the prophet as sent from God. The disturbed Bishop Johnson in his wistful statement seeks to sort out the evil and the good in the movement. He feels it is very perplexing and humbling. He asks for the prayers of the church at home.

Writing some years later, Bishop Lasbrey of the Niger, with whom Bishop Johnson's African successor, Bishop Howells, still works, carries the story of Elijah the Second to its close:

"It was a time of great difficulty for many of the Christians. The prophet, however, was taken up for creating a riot and was imprisoned. One day while doing some work he was struck by lightning and killed. Many of the people, feeling he had been led astray, believed that this was God's judgment upon him, and a number who had left the church returned to it. Others felt he was a martyr.

"There are still in the Niger Delta many congregations which follow his teaching but they have split into two bodies called the Prophet Movement and Christ's Army. In several places large numbers are wanting to return to the church but are reluctant to give up the bad moral customs which the Ba-Malaki have been allowed."

☙ KIBANGU *of the Congo*

The Prophet Movement in the Lower Congo began in 1921. Its leader, Simon Kibangu, is a Christian. Like the stories of many who enter on a prophet's career, his story opens with a vision and a call. Going with his father and his mother (she was a good Christian) to the funeral ceremonies of a friend in another village, he fell into a fit and suffered various vicissitudes. In the course of these a certain stranger appeared to him and spoke to his parents. After his return home and subsequent illness, a stranger appeared again, and more than once, though in a different guise as a meagerly dressed old man full of sores. In a dream he gave Kibangu a Bible and told him to study and teach. He was also bidden to heal a sick child in a neighboring village. He went, laid his hands on the child, and it recovered. This act was accompanied by a violent trembling, which became increasingly characteristic of the similar acts of Kibangu and his followers. From this time on Kibangu prayed and tended many who were ill, and they were healed.

Such exploits could not be hid. Kibangu's fame spread. Multitudes came to him, on their own account and on behalf of their friends. Sufferers were borne to him by any means of transit; he was surrounded night and day by crowds who sought to be healed and taught. As a result of his work a medical mission near him was suspended, all the patients having disappeared, and a hospital that had been crammed to twice its capacity was emptied. He did fail to raise the dead or give sight to the blind, nevertheless his fame and popularity spread, and herein his danger appeared. Those who gathered round him were of divers sorts. Some, with still a glint of light, had been cut off from church membership because of open sin. These and others less taught set up as minor prophets in different villages; the proportion of superstition and evil which marred the movement increased.

Christian Africans, profoundly interested in what was happening, agreed after careful examination that the teaching given by Kibangu was "mixed with deception and distorted." But the feature which finally brought disaster was the anti-white feeling which developed in the movement. Some at least of the minor prophets, if not Kibangu himself, gave out that God would drive the white people out of the country and that taxes need not be paid. Others taught that the return of our Lord was near and that it was needless for people to till their gardens. Famine is never far off in Africa, and the fire of unrest is easily fanned to flame. The Belgian government intervened. There was a tangle of issues hard to unravel, there were trials, sentences and deportations. Kibangu himself was condemned to death, but his sentence was commuted to imprisonment by the Belgian King.

In a large measure this Prophet Movement, like some of the others, has died down. Some of Kibangu's followers are loaded with disappointment, others are still inspired by what they regard as his martyrdom. The Christian church on the Lower Congo has survived the shock; such numbers are seeking baptism that a revival is in progress. Kibangu himself, hurled from notoriety into confinement, remains, one of those who, knowing too little, was borne on to attempt too much.

South African Developments

Many movements, including larger or lesser elements of Christian truth and more or less related to political questions, have arisen in various parts of Africa, such as the Watch Tower Movement in Nyasaland and elsewhere, and that of the Israelites at Bull Hoek near Queenstown in Cape Province. This latter led to a disastrous conflict with the police force in 1921 when the Israelites persisted in refusing to withdraw from land which they unlawfully held.

The story, long and painful, cannot here be told in full. The movement originated in the days of Halley's Comet, when the simple people gathered, in high emotion, on a hillside to await the appearing of the long-tailed star. Then a Native preacher, great in bulk and in stature, Enoch Mgijima by name, proclaimed a new way of approaching and appeasing God. Hope lay in returning to the ancient religion of the patriarchs and worshiping God as they used to do.

The people followed him. Though the New Testament was cut out from the true Bible of God—it was "the white man's fiction which had produced no effect on his life"—the Old Testament remained and was thirstily studied. Many hours of each day were spent in worshiping the Israelites' God.

The movement as it grew strong and found expression developed strange ideas. Steady refusal to obey the civil law became a matter of principle.   Remonstrance from all sides was applied and failed.   Professor D. D. T. Jabavu of Fort Hare (see p. 161) was impressed with the patience and forbearance shown by the government under continued repulse.   At last it was decided that obedience must be enforced.   The Israelites resisted the police force stoutly, and in the fighting which resulted a number of them were killed.   It was lamentable in the extreme. The action of the government was sharply challenged in the Cape Town parliament but was ultimately judged to have been right.   The one good outcome of a most unhappy incident was that it led to the appointment of a commission, first to inquire further into the Bull Hoek affair, and then to inquire into the "nature, origin, and extent" of the bodies known as the separatist churches of South Africa—that is, the churches under purely Native control.

The commission's report [2] throws light on the whole subject of this chapter.   There were found to be between a hundred and twenty and a hundred and forty Native bodies, "ranging from large and well-known churches such as the African Methodist Episcopal Church and the

[2] Summarized by Dr. C. T. Loram in the *International Review of Missions* for July 1927.

African Presbyterian Church, to the many mushroom organizations which spring up and die in the back streets of Johannesburg." These churches the commission found to be separatist rather than heretical, any marked difference of doctrine being rare. There was, however, some reversion to Old Testament ritual, and certain Native customs were introduced. The moral standard was found lower than that of European churches, but immorality was not characteristic of the separatist bodies, nor was a definitely anti-European spirit found.

The report recommended the government to tolerate the movement, in spite of some obvious weaknesses, and to grant civil privileges wherever the churches came up to the standards required for recognition. These, as summarized by Dr. Loram, are: (a) the separate and continuous existence for ten years with signs of development in the shape of a constitution, schools and buildings; (b) a growth extending to six separate congregations, each with its own meeting places; (c) provision for the training of ministers who should ordinarily have had two or three years of special training after passing Standard VI; [3] (d) the conduct of the church

[3] The commission found one Native archbishop whose highest educational qualification was a pass in Standard II.

in accordance with the ordinarily accepted ethical standards; and (e) proof that the ministers are suitable for the exercise of the civil functions of their office.

The commission was of opinion that the separatist movement will grow. Dr. Loram, having noted the action of the United Free Church of Scotland in approving the formation of the Bantu Presbyterian church in which white missionaries sit under a black Moderator, and the increasing freedom of action granted by the Church of the Province of South Africa and the Wesleyan church to their Native members, anticipates that the Native churches will "in the end separate themselves more or less completely from the European churches, while desiring and indeed retaining cordial relations with them." He adds these sane and hopeful words: "This is but a natural evolution for the Native church, and there seems no reason to regret the development of great African churches charged with a special mission to take spiritual care of the African peoples."

The Making of Prophets

What is the interpretation of this African religious activity, marked by independence and at times identified with racial revolt, ranging from sporadic movements born in Liberia, in Uganda, in the Niger Delta and on the Congo, to certain extremes in some of the separatist bodies in South Africa?

Human nature has everywhere been inclined to find expression in sects; the separatist churches of South Africa are not without parallel elsewhere. But the genuine African prophet, while a familiar figure in pagan tribes,[4] stands alone in church history. Nowhere else has the introduction of Christianity among animistic peoples—or among those of ancient book religions, for the matter of that—brought out a crop of Native Christian leaders so ignorant, so sincere, and so successful until some catastrophe, whether banishment or prison, has cut short their career.

It is of course quite easy to gather up failings, as one gathers stones from the surface of a field, to make missiles for those who would stone the prophets once more. But the soil which has bred these men remains and will breed more. The real question is how to cultivate rather than what to condemn. It matters intensely that the church should learn why African prophets in

[4] For a graphic sketch of several such prophets, see *The Ila-Speaking Peoples of Northern Rhodesia*, by E. W. Smith and A. M. Dale, 2 vols., Macmillan Company, New York, 1920.

the past were what they were, and how in the future they may become what they might be.

Some who have been among the prophets are at a loss to interpret them and their ways. Thus Archdeacon Blackledge of Uganda writes: "What was the real origin of the Malakite movement? Was it sheer crankiness based on a single text? Was it a sincere desire to arouse a true and simple faith in God? The ready acceptance of polygamy seems a negation of that. Or was it an anti-white movement, black against white, African against European? I frankly cannot tell."

Dr. P. H. J. Lerrigo of New York, who was in the midst of the Kibangu movement when it was at its height, is prepared to go further in explanation. "The whole agitation would seem to indicate a new and growing sense of solidarity and African race consciousness which must be reckoned with in future; a desire for leadership, a willingness to pay the price of leadership, and, at least to some extent, a capacity for leadership which can and indubitably should be capitalized for the Kingdom of God."

African prophets in the flesh are far from the readers of these pages, but it may be worth while to group the facts which have been stated and see what light comparative study gives.

William Wadé Harris stands apart from the others by virtue of his simplicity, his lack of self-consciousness or conceit, his readiness to yield rather than oppose. His message carries him rather than he it. His purity of motive, his bodily discipline, his patient continuance in well-doing, make his work unique in Africa, perhaps in the world. He has no education, he does not discern the deeper manifestations of God, his mental horizon is cramped, though clear with the light of heaven. He could not have worked in concert with Malaki or Garrick or Kibangu. In his active days he was wise as a serpent; now in his seaside hut he is harmless as a dove. A great content has always been his.

Malaki, still smaller in mental horizon, has a spirit inclined to be self-righteous and contentious. His type is not unknown. He can storm a mission hospital or loudly rebuke one of his fathers in God. The "anti" spirit of the illiterate reformer is his. He has fixed ideas which will not mate with the ideas of others, so there is no birth of new thought in his mind. He can condone moral laxness but never difference of belief. He is eager to proclaim the motley fragments which he conceives to be the whole of truth; he welcomes a fight.   Yet he has remained simple and sincere.

Elijah the Second, from the lowly and diligent service of his small beginnings, soon moves into the sphere of the popular prophet and accepts the gross adulation he is given.   He uses force and fear to combat idolatry, where Harris used the influence of truth however small his stock.   He is fiercely moral about drink but allows polygamy.   He inculcates confession, prayer and worship—of a mechanical kind.   He accepts for himself what Harris or Malaki would have rejected.   There is something of pose here which makes one turn back to the arid reality of Malaki with relief.

Kibangu in his short term of prophetic office had amazing success.   He too trod the downward path of adulation.   He quickly—too quickly for safety—multiplied himself.   His assistant prophets drifted into the political whirlpools.   Kibangu went with them and was lost to sight.

Undoubtedly, as the men are seen grouped together, Dr. Lerrigo is right.   There is here capacity for leadership (all the more marked because intellectual equipment is lacking).   Not one of the prophets was deserted; they were re-moved. The continuance of Harris's work after his deportation is one of the marvels of religious history.

There are few things in the chronicles of the expansion of Christendom which summon more imperiously to thought than this flight of Afri-can prophets—eager, full of enterprise, leaders among their fellows, impelled by dreams and visions to tell forth what they believe, suscep-tible to foibles and pose and human passions, without the education which enlarges the mind and the discipline which controls desire, wasting what might have been splendid evangelism in the blind alleys of heresy and schism. These men are more arresting to the imagination of some than are great Africans like Khama or Ag-grey. They start from the back of nowhere with hosts of followers behind them, and push ahead till they vanish in banishment or in prison. It is easy to fling stones at them; the stones in abundance are there. But what matters is that the church should learn how to use her prophet-children who have in them that urge of leader-ship which their fellows recognize.

It is not easy to catch a prophet and remake him. Once the mantle falls on his shoulders he must run his own course. But if the prophetic aspect of the African's nature is recognized and studied, provision for its nurture and discipline may be made in home and school, and room be found for its expression within the recognized fold of the church.

To the African, religion is the great reality which permeates all life. The prophet can only be prepared, as it were, in advance if he is dealt with *in situ*, if the Christian way of life and the power to live it are brought near to the rank and file of the people to which by origin he belongs. Some points arising in the stories of the prophets illustrate this.

Obviously the use of the Bible is one point. The late Professor Maurice Delafosse, one of the great French Islamists, found that the intense interest of the Africans in a book was one of the reasons why Islam drew the pagan. Bookless themselves, without any written traditions for the conduct of their lives, it is natural that the Africans should find satisfaction in a written code of rules. Too often the unlettered inquirer among them grasps at the Bible as if it were a charm or a fetish, and at its letters and words as if they were spirit and gave life. The prophets lost themselves in some measure thus; in the obscurantist use of texts; in adoption of Old Testament ritual and morals; in a view of Jehovah veiled in gloom and wrath, avenging himself by dire catastrophe; in cutting out the New Testament as only a white man's book.

What the African needs is no final Koranic code. He needs to learn of a revelation which flows like a river of God down the ages, growing in depth and volume as it flows, ever fed by fresh springs of the spirit enriching the minds of men. When the Old Testament is so taught to the African that he sees the dawn which begins with the patriarchal stories, akin in form and color to his daily life, brightening century by century into the full light of that gospel day in which by grace he stands, then will those cherished ancient records cease to be a stumbling block, and become for him, as they were to the Son of Man himself, a ladder of truth. Is the Bible always so taught?

Quite as clearly the place of faith in the make-up of the African prophet challenges thought. To the Africans, the simple unlettered people to whom prophets are kin, faith is natural and unquestioned. An African, educated or uneducated, cannot conceive life apart from belief in God and the unseen. With amazement Mr.

John Dube, one of the African members of the Belgian conference (see p. 5), heard, when visiting London, an atheist addressing an interested audience in Hyde Park. "No one would listen to him in Africa," he said.

The repression of faith causes disease in the soul. The church in the West is slow to experiment with mountains. To the African, faith is more real than mountains, and within the small orbit of his experience his experiments work out. Where the church in the West is only beginning to recover faith in spiritual healing, the African, through the dim and dusty mazes of incantation and witch doctor, has been there all the time.

He had had his herbal remedies, and some of them are good, but the real cure as he sees it lies in the region of the spirit world. With the splendid gift to Africa of hospitals, doctors and nurses, with the triumphs of research and preventive medicine, the church must enter also into the African's view of the nearness of the spirit to the bodily world. Was it only a misunderstanding of Scripture which led the African prophets to lay stress on spiritual healings? Was it not also a hungry faith? And when faith hungers for outlet, it hurts more than does craving for bodily food. Is there any reason why the church should not indent fully upon this reservoir of capacity to believe, not only for the needs of the body, but for the needs of the home, of the community, of the church itself, of Africa, of the world? It would be worth while to make inquiry as to what provision is made for the education and enlightenment of the African's gift of faith, what exercise of faith is habitual in the life of church and school.

Once more, it is tragic and instructive to see how the moral standard of the prophet is often—not always—inclined to drop below that of the church. There is some restraint which is intolerable either to him or to his followers, and from it he breaks away or at least releases them. Against idolatry and against strong drink he is vehement; polygamy he condones. It is in the schools where the prophets are in training that the church must deal with this situation.

To the African, human nature is strong and natural desires are clamant. Even the prophet is no cold man of the West—if such there really be. He inherits a tradition of licence, he is bred to a social order where women are the slaves of men. The thousand influences of home and clan and tribe are against him; the burden of field work is too heavy for one woman alone; the plea of justice for other wives already taken is not lightly to be put aside. No frail bar of prohibition, no urging of isolated texts, no withholding of baptism from the polygamist, will lift prophet or followers to those high paths of Christian purity which Khama and Dr. Aggrey trod and believed to be possible for their race. For adult Africans brought late in life into the church the way is inevitably hard. What can be done for the future prophets?

Young Africa today is in school and college, for the most part under care of the church. It is only by changing young Africa that African custom can be changed.

Is it possible to conceive of a school through which a future prophet might pass, to come out freed from obscurantism, from the "anti" spirit of unbalanced faith, from the moral weakness or social cowardice which practises or condones polygamy—and yet be a son of the prophets still? Yes; but girls as well as boys, women as well as men, must know the care of the church.

What about a school, whether village or central, with such characteristics as these that follow?— Filled with the influence of Christian personality; character called out through service of others and trained in the ways of life;

opportunity clear for faith to test itself against mountains, a spirit of adventure adding zest to the air; the facts of life faced with pure simplicity, its mysteries of birth explored in the plant and animal worlds; Christian forms of Native customs making for the discipline of early manhood and womanhood; intercourse between young people of both sexes a happy natural part of life; chivalry taught not by injunction but by letting the strong taste the joy of caring for the weak; mother-love and mothercraft as an introduction to holy motherhood; private prayer, communion with God and his united worship as the central privilege of each day—all this set in an atmosphere of hard work in classroom, workshop, garden and playing field—if such equipment there be—linked at every turn with community life, soaked in the lore of Africa—this is the sort of school where African sons and daughters of the prophets might be trained as leaders for the future.

There are such schools in Africa. Why are there not many more?

XIII. MOTHERS OF MEN

"ONLY one chapter—and that one at the close —about African women." But is this really so? Look through the previous pages and note the part played by the wives and mothers of men. Bishop Crowther rediscovering Afala his mother, happy in fifty years of wedded life with Susan his wife; Tshaka with his mother Nandi who never failed her son; Moshesh taking the first missionary to visit his favorite wife Mamahoto; Khama, from the beauty of his home life, first with Ma-Bessie and then with Semane, learning to extend to other women a brother's protecting care; John Tengo Jabavu, with Mary Mpindi his hard-working mother, and Elda his devoted wife; James Kwegyir Aggrey, with a home in two continents, believer in African woman- hood—through all of these, women have already crossed and recrossed our stage. Now the time has come when the women of Africa step into the center to be studied more at leisure and ap- preciated to the full.

All Sorts and Conditions of Women

There are the queen-mothers, through whom passes the royal line, influential alike in court life, in religion, and in family affairs. Speke had to pay as much attention in Uganda to the queen-mother as to Mutesa the king. In his anthropological work in Ashanti Captain Rattray found the queen-mothers the best sources of information, and made them his loyal friends.

There are the women warriors, like the fierce Amazons of Dahomey whose bodies Bishop Crowther found strown round Abeokuta after the defeat of their king, and like Ma-Ntatesi, leader of the Mantatis, one of the products of Tshaka's wars. Ma-Ntatesi was chieftainess of the Batlakoa tribe of which her son Sekonyela was chief. She was a tall slender woman, tawny rather than black, with features more Asiatic than African, and cold eyes that could command men. Her own tribe, shattered by another tribe which was fleeing before Tshaka, served as nucleus for other broken tribes, until at last a vast horde of despairing people moved, under this woman's leadership, in masses which darkened whole hillsides, striking terror where they went. The cry, "The Mantatis are coming," sent men flying to shelter if shelter could be found. Ma-Ntatesi became a legendary person as wild rumors spread through the distracted land: she was said to be of gigantic stature, with one eye in the middle of her forehead; she sent swarms of hornets before her armies, and when her soldiers hungered she fed them with her own milk.

At last, after a battle with the Griquas and their allies which was witnessed by Dr. Robert Moffat, the great missionary from Kuruman, the ranks of the Mantatis were broken up and never regained full power. Parts of the host went in different directions; some died of starvation; Ma-Ntatesi and her son Sekonyela continued to harass the regions round the Caledon River; Moshesh had to do with them, as has been told.

There are also the women chiefs and ruling queens. One of the groups that broke off from the Mantatis had a young leader named Sebituane, who with magnificent courage and resource pushed northward to the Zambesi. When Livingstone visited him at Linyanti he had built up the Makololo empire. With the remembrance, possibly, of Ma-Ntatesi, he trained his daughter Mamochisane to succeed him. She was given a district to govern, that thus she might learn how to rule; she had to live as did a chief; because chiefs had many wives she must have many husbands. The other women took vigorous exception to the idea, and Mamochisane made up her mind that it was better to be a woman than a chief. Sebituane suddenly died when Livingstone was staying at Linyanti. Livingstone left for Cape Town before the succession was arranged, and when he returned he found that Mamochisane had persistently refused to be chief, thrusting the responsibility upon her reluctant younger brother Sekeleku and returning to her district again. Livingstone did his best to guide Sekeletu but he was weak and irresolute, and by degrees his great empire waned.

In one of his journals Livingstone, who noted with humorous eye the professional dignity of the women witch doctors and the successful ruses by which the weak overcame the strong, tells of the wife of a local chief who temporarily traveled under his care. Camping near some Native huts one evening he heard a woman in loud complaint, and found she had been captured and was going to be sold as a slave. Her captors were not having an easy time; she had a poor opinion of them and let her views be known. Livingstone intervened on her behalf: to steal a chief's wife meant war; was the woman worth it? At last prudence gained the day and she was released. But again the loud complaints arose, this time with added insistence. Her ornaments had been taken from her; go home without them she would not. Into her captor's hut she went, recounting the sum of her belongings, nor did she leave nor drop her voice till all were hers again. On the march there was some trouble with the carriers; she promptly picked up a man's load of beads, put it on her head, and went forward.

One of the quaintest and most effective of African potentates was Indhlovu-kasi (Female Elephant), queen of Swaziland.[1] For more than thirty years she was a paramount influence in Swaziland during the reign of her good husband Mbandine, her dissolute son Mbundu, and the long minority of her grandson Buzza. Only in 1922, at the instance of the British Government, did she resign her power into the young king's hands. She was the daughter of a small chief who was "smelled out" as a wizard; the girl was taken by Mbandine to wait upon his wives and ended by becoming chief wife and

[1] *Dawn in Swaziland*, by O. C. Watts; S. P. G., London, 1922.

queen. She was an able woman with remarkable memory and shrewd judgment; neither with white men nor with Swazis was she ever at a loss. At the time of the Boer War she is said to have held her own in discussions with Lord Milner, the Earl of Selborne, and agents both Dutch and British.

"During the Great War," writes Archdeacon Watts, "the mayor of Johannesburg visited Swaziland and called on the queen. . . . On arriving at the Royal Kraal the old queen asked him who he was and where he came from. He answered that he was mayor of Johannesburg, and had lately been busy raising recruits for the war. 'From Johannesburg?' said the queen. 'I do not hear much good of it, and if you want recruits for the war, being a big fat man, why don't you go yourself?' The mayor changed the conversation. 'This friend of mine is a surveyor and brings water in pipes to the town,' he said. 'When I want water I make rain myself,' answered the queen."

This notable woman lived in dirt and squalor. Her kraal was untidy and insanitary. When visited she would be found lying on the ground in her hut, clad only in a well-greased skin apron, her gray woolly hair plastered with clay on the top of her head and bound with charms, a pot of beer and some snuff beside her for refreshment. One hand would wave an oxtail to keep off flies, in the other would be a wooden scraper for scratching herself. Yet even in the midst of such surroundings her dignity and ability made themselves felt. Though the old forces ruled in her kraal, she sought peace and supported the government.

Here is another story told by Archdeacon Watts which shows the Female Elephant among her Swazis.

A terrible drought visited Swaziland. Large deputations visited the queen not only from Swaziland but from other parts of the country, to implore her to make rain. The old queen replied that she was tired and not inclined to make it. But if they gave her enough cattle and enough yellow money, she might be persuaded . . . Larger and more desperate deputations went to her from week to week. "You are hard-hearted, O Indhlovu-kasi, our cattle will soon be dead, there are no mealies. Make rain, you starve us all." But the old queen remained in her hut. . . . The deputations, made bold by despair, changed entreaties to threats. "You are old and useless and cannot make the rain. You must die, and your daughter-in-law, a more effective rainmaker, be put in your place."

The old queen knew that she must act. "You must bring me black cattle from a place six days off," she said. They arrived, but she let two days pass before she went to see them. "These cattle have white marks upon them, and I asked for black," she said. "Take them back and bring me black." In the double journey another twelve days passed. Rain could not hold off much longer. "Take them back where they came from, and as they reach home I will make you rain," she said. And sure enough, in six days rain began.

But, as often happens, the drought ended in a deluge. The rivers overflowed their banks, mealie gardens were washed away, great damage was done. The deputations came again. "Indhlovu-kasi, you are more cruel than ever. You starved us before, now you kill us." "It is a punishment," she answered. "I did not want to make rain and you forced me to do it. Now I shall not stop it, and it will teach you not to trouble me again at inconvenient times."

The women known to history, or in heathen courts and kraals, are not more worthy of study than are the African women who have been under Christian influence in recent years. Mabel Shaw of Mbereshi in Northern Rhodesia has sketched life in her school village in lines as delicate and as sure as those in which Jean Kenyon Mackenzie has limned her African women

friends in Cameroun.[2]   Against unfathomable
depths of shadow exquisite forms of childhood
and womanhood stand out, now in the hard light
of suffering, now in the soft light of human love
and joy.

Here only two stories illustrative of the qualities of African women can be told.

ℱ The Story of RAKERI

Sleeping sickness was rife round the shores of
the Victoria Nyanza.   The fishermen were almost extinct; some of the islands were depopu-
lated.   In the infected areas gardens fell out of
cultivation, houses sank into ruins, churches
were closed; the frenzied ravings of stricken people, the death-wail of mourners, and the night
howl of hyenas searching for dead bodies filled
the air.   The Angel of Death hovered over the
land.   Science, of course, got to work with research and experiment.   Preventive measures
were actively set on foot by the government and
the missionaries.   But it was long before sure
ways of fighting the disease were found; indeed,

[2] See, for Miss Shaw's work, the Phelps-Stokes report, *Education in East
Africa*, p. 308, and the *International Review of Missions*, October 1925.   Of
Miss Mackenzie's books on life in Cameroun the best known are *An African
Trail*, *Black Sheep*, and *African Clearings*.

the battle still wages, though victory seems in sight.

There was, so Bishop Tucker tells us, in the congregation at Ngogwe on the shores of the lake a woman named Rakeri (Rachel) whose heart was stirred on hearing of a certain island where sleeping sickness was upon the people. There was no one to care for the dying or teach the way of truth. Rakeri volunteered to go to the women and children, though at the risk of life. She knew infection meant death. She went, and came back after a time well and thankful, telling how her service had been welcomed and her message heard. She went again. A few months later came news that she was ill. She was brought to the mission hospital in Mengo; the dread verdict, "sleeping sickness," was pronounced.

For months Rakeri, full of life and love, trod the slow approach to death. In the hospital, where she remained under treatment and care, she was a ministering angel in the women's ward. From bed to bed she passed, entirely self-forgetful, soothing those in pain, reading to those who would listen, praying where she found an open mind. While strength remained she would creep to the holy communion in the cathedral near the hospital, sit in a distant corner, and come forward alone, with slow and dragging steps, when other communicants had gone.

When the final stages of fatal slumber were on her the bishop himself came and stood by her bed. A flicker of the eyelids showed that perhaps she knew he was there. He bent and whispered in her ear the blessing of the Father and of the Son and of the Holy Ghost.

"Where," he asks, and in truth we ask it with him, "in the whole history of the Christian church is there to be found a nobler instance of self-sacrificing love?"

The Story of MAMA EKILA

Ekila was born about forty years ago, far up country on a tributary of the Congo River. She was a slave girl, not by capture but by birth. She was passed from one man to another of her own people. Her last owner came down the river to Brazzaville looking for work. He died there, and by French law in that region Ekila was free. She took up with a sorry individual named Blackiman and after some form of marriage lived with him as his wife.

Among their friends was a young man, a baptized Christian, who had done wrong and been dismissed from the service of the English Baptist Mission. He was wont to tell the gospel story; Ekila heard it and longed to know more.

The mighty Congo, passing through Stanley Pool as it rolls onward to the ocean, has Brazzaville the French capital on the one bank, and Kinshasa in Belgian territory just opposite. Ekila could see the mission station across the river; she could even hear the drum that called the men and boys to morning prayer. She persuaded Blackiman to look for work in Kinshasa; then she went and sat on a mat with the little ones in school, learned to read the New Testament, joined the inquirers' class, and in 1908 she was baptized.

Then Ekila started a little school under a baobab tree, with no equipment but a few slates and reading cards. The missionaries began to teach her how to give help to women at the time of childbirth; a woman doctor came and taught her more. Soon Ekila was in request by day and by night. She was called off to distant villages and would come back leaving mother and baby well. She learned how to deal with difficult cases and had extraordinary success. Even the Portuguese women sought her aid.

Ekila adopted a little ailing derelict boy whom

she found on a dust heap and lavished on him her mother love. Moswe grew to be a healthy lad. She had not much happiness with Blackiman, who drank heavily and expected her to support him. He went off to look for work and sent her no money and finally came back with another woman and looked to Ekila to house and feed them both. Things grew so bad that the government officer declared that Ekila was free to leave her husband, and she went with Moswe to the mission house. When Blackiman fell ill with sleeping sickness Ekila did all she could to feed and care for him until he was taken to the segregation village where he died. She really loved the worthless man.

The population of Kinshasa was growing as trade increased. Temptations for girls and women were many. Ekila had a second room in her little home where she took in women and cared for them; here many healthy babies were born. A fierce epidemic of influenza, followed by an outbreak of infantile paralysis, swept through Kinshasa. Ekila stood by the medical staff, won the people to trust the preventive measures, and saved many lives.

Intelligent and eager to learn, Ekila had become proficient in her difficult work. An eminent Belgian doctor came to study the causes of infant mortality in the Colony. The missionaries told him of Ekila and he asked to see her alone. She was out at a case in the village, and he followed her to the hut and stood watching her and her ways as she cared for the mother and helped another little life into the world. Afterwards this Belgian scientist wrote to the mission: "If Ekila had been a white woman I should certainly have felt justified in giving her a certificate to practise in the Colony."

One morning the mission house was startled by the news that Ekila had been arrested and was in prison, charged by a man with killing his child at its birth. The charge being definite, the officers of police had to act; Ekila was shut up all night in a room with three men arrested on a murder charge. Gradually peace came back to her; she sang hymns and told her companions of Jesus. The missionaries saw the chief of police; they engaged the best advocate in Kinshasa, and with him saw the judge, who knew Ekila well. The women gathered round the police station holding up their babies. They sent for the police officer and cried, "These are her babies; if you put her in prison who will look after us?" Scores of women, pagan and Christian, Protestant and Roman Catholic, flocked to the mission house declaring that they would go to the court with their babies if Ekila were put on trial and demand her release.

It was the Roman Catholic priest's intervention which availed. He knew Ekila and had wanted her to join his church. He sought out the man who had accused her, decided that the charge was false, gave the man a good thrashing, and went to tell the doctor what he had found out. Ekila was questioned and set free with apologies. The judge personally offered his sympathy, the advocate never sent in his bill, the police were more than ever on her side, the Christians met to give thanks for answered prayer.

So Ekila's life of service has gone on, and goes on still. She is an effective Bible teacher in her own way. She is frequently consulted by the judge on Native matters, especially in family disputes. She is a companion and friend to the women missionaries. She often sleeps in the house of white residents in Kinshasa when the men of the family are away on business.

The missionary Ekila specially loved was leaving Kinshasa. Good-bys had been said at home; Ekila would not go to the station lest she should break down. Then she remembered that other women would be sorrowful, so she went. There outside the fence stood a crowd of women, just as she expected, crying and making a noise. Ekila was last seen lending them her handkerchief and wiping the tears from their eyes, forgetting herself.

❦ Dr. Aggrey's View

No more fitting close can be found for this chapter than a summary of the point of view of Dr. Aggrey with regard to African women.

In his early school days at Cape Coast Castle he saw the missionary start one sunny day across the courtyard without a hat. The missionary's wife saw it too, and called her husband back in gentle insistent tones. He hesitated, yielded, and returned for his hat. The boy, who saw the significance of the action and the relationship which underlay it, said to himself, "When I have a wife, I will treat her like that." He kept his word.

In his American days, as he loved to recount, he knew the full partnership of a woman's mind. He and his wife sat in class together during summer sessions and delighted their professors by vigorously taking opposite sides. He often told how at the end of a long day's work his wife would cook him a good dinner, tidy the house, see to the welfare of the children, and then sit down to discuss with him educational methods or English literature or some question of the hour.

As professor at Achimota he sought out records of notable women, that they might be given equal place in his lectures on African history with notable men. He held that not only the education of women but the education of men with regard to women was one of Africa's greatest needs.

He cherished the best in the tribal ways regarding women, and vehemently attacked the worst. He valued, for instance, the place accorded to women by virtue of their work in field and garden, though in modern days, when areas of cultivation are wider and standards of domestic comfort are rising, he would see more of the heavier work transferred to the men. He saw in motherhood the glory of an African woman's life, and in the care of children her highest service. But, with Khama, he was unshakable as to the evils of polygamy and the blessings which faithful Christian marriage brought for both woman and man.

The initiation ceremonies, whether for girls

or boys, he saw as a faulty road towards a true
ideal; he saw danger in their disappearance and
would have welcomed some Christian substitute
to take their place. With unerring instinct he
divided things which were worthily national and
characteristic from those which were trivial or
superstitious or impure. In all that bore on the
customary relation of the sexes in Africa he took
forth the precious from the vile as none but an
enlightened Christian African could do.

He believed in higher, or rather in the highest,
education for women, but never put a professional career for them before married life. It
was his hope that African women graduates
might find that they could devote a few years to
teaching or hospital work in their own country
before setting up a home of their own.

In an opinion antedating the Phelps-Stokes
Commission, Dr. Aggrey went all the way with
the reports of the two Commissions as to the
education of women. Possibly he went a little
farther in wanting for African women a fuller
enrichment through all that makes for beauty
and culture—literature, art, music—in the
sphere of domestic and social life. With humorous heat he was wont to insist that the education of African women would be shaped by

themselves alone; they were beginning to know what they wanted, and what they wanted they would ultimately get. He saw in coming days, and not on any far horizon, well-educated African women bringing into their national heritage the best treasures of the West, partners in thought as in work with their husbands, good wives, good mothers, good thinkers, with a thread of beauty woven by them into daily life.

More than most Africans, Dr. Aggrey knew white women who counted him as a friend. He honored them with frank and simple courtesy. But in the women of his own race he saw qualities which equally held his respect and reverence; it was the marriage of African with African, and the upbringing of African children in African homes, which inspired him with hope for the partnership of his people in the affairs of men.

XIV. TO CONCLUDE—

THE present book deals almost entirely with completed lives, and does not include in its records the many capable, educated younger Africans who are now becoming known. They have recently made their voice heard in the sincere and arresting statement of the modern situation in the book entitled *Thinking with Africa,* planned by the Student Volunteer Movement and published in America by the Missionary Education Movement and in Great Britain by the Student Christian Movement. Under the strong stimulus of situations more complex and more disturbing than those of even Jabavu's day, the young Africans seek after larger opportunities. Some are already finding noble outlet in community service, in interracial organizations, in labor movements, and in other forms of enterprise. Some are still impeded by limitations in their way. There are white men standing by them—from America, from Europe, from South Africa—in brotherly sympathy, coveting for them a life full of the freedom of those who serve God and their fellow-men.

It may be that the stories of eminent Africans here told may bear upon a present situation so poignant for all concerned. Here may be seen a little of what Africans have done and therefore can do—a medicine for doubting minds. Here too may be marked the steps which have led Africans to success: patience, industry, courage, resourcefulness; a cordial for those who falter as they face so steep a way. Here, once more, may be seen worked out in life that gospel of cooperation—the many fingers on the one hand, the black and white notes which together make human music—which is today more than ever the hope of the races of Africa and of the world.

plenary
corollary